The Kashmir Residency

The author in Kashmir, 1940

The Kashmir Residency

Memories of 1939 and 1940

by
Evelyn Désirée Battye

BACSA
PUTNEY, LONDON
1997

Published by the British Association
for Cemeteries in South Asia (BACSA)

Secretary: Theon Wilkinson MBE
76½ Chartfield Avenue
London SW15 6HQ

The British Association for Cemeteries in South Asia was formed in 1976 to
preserve, convert and record old European cemeteries.
All proceeds from the sale of this book go towards this charity
(Registered No 273422)

ISBN 0 907799 59 0

British Libraries Cataloguing-in-Publication Data
A catalogue record for this book is available from the British Library

Typeset by Professional Presentation, 3 Prairie Road, Addlestone, Surrey

Printed by The Chameleon Press Ltd., 5-25 Burr Road, Wandsworth SW18 4SG

Contents

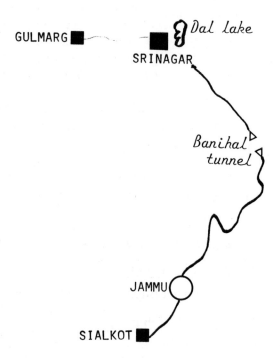

Wulan lake

GULMARG

Dal lake

SRINAGAR

Banihal tunnel

JAMMU

SIALKOT

LAHORE

AMRITSAR

Scale 1": 25 miles (approx.)

Foreword

The Kashmir Residency is the twenty-seventh in a series of books about Europeans in South Asia, written by BACSA members, published by BACSA for BACSA members with a wider public in mind. This book, set in the 1939-40 period, will appeal to many of those who have visited the 'enchanted Vale of Kashmir' or are interested in the inner life of a British Residency pre-Independence.

The buildings, the rooms and gardens are minutely described along with the calendar of events that took place from Garden Parties entertaining the Maharaja of Kashmir, to shikar on the higher hills and fishing in the valleys. The 'Residency' in its widest sense covered the main house in Srinagar, the *summer* lodge in Gulmarg, and the old *winter* bungalow in Sialkot, with intimate descriptions of the life and work in each. The existence of a Kashmir Residency in Sialkot - now in Pakistan - underlines the complications in the later political situation.

The author is already well-known to BACSA members from her book *The Fighting Ten*, the story of the Battye brothers; ten members of a Victorian family who became celebrated for their deeds of valour in British India and Afghanistan. But this is a purely personal account, drawn from the letters and diaries of her two exciting years in Kashmir, from the time she joined as Personal Assistant to the Resident, to the seemingly fore-ordained 'entanglement' with a Battye. This was Stuart Hedley Molesworth Battye, later Major-General, RE, CB, MA, FRSA an enthusiastic supporter of BACSA until his death in 1987. He came out to India in 1930, after passing through the Royal Military Academy and Cambridge, and then joined the Bengal Sappers and Miners being posted almost immediately to operations on the North-West Frontier.

After the war, the author continued to 'pack and follow' round the world until her husband retired and she settled down to write. Her first book was *Costumes and Characters of the British Raj*. Since then she has produced a steady stream of magazine articles, a historical novel and a number of romantic novels, mostly set in the East; the novels under her pen-name Evelyn Hart. Details of her main publications are given on the back cover.

To my grandchildren
with love

1
Queen of Cities

Early in the morning the *SS Tairea* slowly made her way through the narrows at Kolaba Point into Bombay's vast land-bound harbour. It was 1939 but there was no visible sign of the war which had recently broken out in Europe and had caused a flurry of cables to and from Kenya where the men were being called up leaving their women-folk to run the farms. 'Do you still want me? Shall I cancel my passage?' The welcome answer arrived pronto: 'Come as arranged. We carry on as usual.'

Certainly the scene in harbour could not have looked more peaceful with ships quietly at anchor. They were a mixture of rusting cargo boats, and the spotless grey of HM Far Eastern Fleet, the latter's crews in white uniform. Prosperous looking passengers crowded the decks of P & O liners to view the dawn as crimson streaks lit up the flat roofs and towers of the city. Small craft laden with fruit and vegetables scurried by on the calm muddy-coloured waters.

From my vantage point on deck I watched our ship being manoeuvred into position by Ballard Pier. Far below on the dockside a teeming crowd of noisy humanity had gathered, and for the first time the excitement at having arrived became tempered by the nagging doubt that I, a lone and admittedly nervous traveller, could get through this initial crowd, let alone travel thousands of miles on to the northern ends of the continent of India.

The interminable wait that followed the docking only increased my apprehension as my shipmates vanished, most of them led chattering away by friends and relatives who had arrived up on deck. I had been informed that someone would meet me, but where was he and how on earth would I recognise him or he me? During the wait I was told to take my turn to be examined by an Eurasian Inspector of Health, a dark little man in a white coat who had the unenviable task of examining hundreds of pairs of sweating feet. I gathered that before allowing passengers from East Africa to set foot in India this search was made for chiggars, horrible insects that burrowed under toenails and laid eggs which when ripe had to be painfully extracted.

'How do they do it?' I looked down at the man at my feet. Ghoulishly I imagined whole toenails or even toes removed should the little beasts be discovered.

'With needle burnt blue in flame of match,' he readily responded, 'but you, Madam, are all clear!' And he waved me aside to queue for more interrogations with doctors and immigration officials. At last, clutching my small luggage, I was permitted to descend the gangway and face the hubbub below. I presumed that whoever was supposed to meet me on board had given up.

Once on the dock the heat and smell of India hit me as if from a hot blast of an open oven door, a blast which contained a richly spiced malodorous stew. I found myself surrounded by hordes of beggars crowding me in a great surge of shouts for cash: '*Baksheesh, Memsahib. Baksheesh, baksheesh, ek paisa do*, give one *pice*....' outstretched brown hands demanded. I was horrified by the sight of some showing stumps where hands and feet should have been. Many were children with fly-encrusted eyelids; others were so lacking in limbs that they had to propel their truncated bodies on roughly made wooden trollies.

When I fumbled for my purse, the press increased. In Africa on my journey out it had not been like this. There the natives had kept a respectful distance, and there the heat was sticky and steamy. Here, engulfed by the very numbers, I stood helplessly imprisoned, panic setting in, any initial impulse of finding some coins gone, all brave ideas of exploring the city discarded. My only wish was to escape as quickly as I could from the ragged, foetid crush. Somehow I must get myself to the station where I would spend the day in the safety of a ladies waiting room till it was time to catch my evening train.

Carried by the jabbering crowd, I was propelled to a large tin-roofed warehouse. Once in with the sun beating down on the roof it was more like being *inside* the aforesaid oven. Even with a Cox and King's representative who arrived to help, it took two hours to find my heavy luggage - a large square hat-box; a big tin-lined wooden box designed against moth and silver fish; and a two-tiered 'Wanted on Voyage' trunk. By the time I had got through the chaos of the Customs, I despaired of even reaching the station, and began to see why the great frontier express did not leave until late in the day. Then, while waiting in a daze beside all my clobber, I heard an authoritative voice above the bedlam.

'*Hat-jao, hat-jao, chup-rao, chalo chalo* - shut up and be off with you!' the voice declaimed. As if by magic the crowd parted by the exit to allow through a tall fierce-looking Indian, 'move away there. Get on with it - hurry!' the man waved his hands. 'Hart Miss-sahib?' he haughtily enquired as he came up to me.

I nodded suspiciously. Who was he? How did he know my name? I was not going to trust anyone after the buffeting I had received. The man raised his right hand, palm inwards to his *pugri* and slightly bowed his head and shoulders all in one graceful movement. He handed me a large buff envelope embossed with a gold coat-of-arms.

After completing a secretarial course in London I had travelled out, with long stops in South Africa and Kenya, to take up the job of PA (personal assistant) to the Resident in Kashmir. I tore the envelope open and recognized the writing of the lady of the house whom I had previously known in England. 'Welcome to India,' I read. 'My own bearer, Dost Mohammed, will escort you on the journey. He speaks some English. You can trust him with your life!'

2

'I make all *bundobast* Miss-sahib,' Dost Mohammed declared. With an imperious gesture he summoned from out of the throng two porters in khaki wearing official red arm bands. I was only too grateful to leave all to him and in no time found myself plucked by this employee of the Raj - who to my mind in no measure of the word could be called a 'servant' - with whom my status was miraculously transformed from an alarmed non-entity to one of the 'heaven-borns'. These high-ups came directly under the Viceroy, the King's representative in India. The Raj ruler was the King Emperor George VI himself, the Kaiser-i-Hind, who not only ruled India but half the world as well. I had previously been instructed in the set-up and told that without the goodwill, industry, honesty and loyal application of the Indian civil servants the British could not have governed so vast a country. Virtually the Indians were perfectly capable of governing themselves, and Independence had been drawing near when War struck to put all on hold for the duration. This was British India. But I was destined for one of the Princely States ruled by its hereditary Maharaja where the British representative was known as a 'Resident', equivalent to an ambassador with consular duties in a foreign country, and with only limited power.

I examined my rescuer. He was an elderly man, from the North Western border I learned, a Muslim with handlebar moustache, a man of great dignity and seriousness who seldom smiled even when pulling my leg, as I soon found out he liked to do! His obeisance as he had greeted me had not in the least lowered the loftiness of his bearing which, had I not had evidence that he had come to take care of me, could have been quite alarming with his hawk-like narrow nose and eagle-glinting sceptical black eyes. It was made clear to me right from the beginning that although he probably *would* guard me with his life, it was really beneath him to look after someone so lowly as a Miss-sahib of no standing. The man wore the dress of white pyjama trousers covered by a long collarless shirt with brown waistcoat over. On his head was a spotless white *pugri* slashed by the red and gold ribbon of the Residency colours.

'The Colonel and his lady are well?' I enquired. '*Bahut accha*,' Dost Mohammed replied shortly. He bundled me and my things into an ancient bull-nosed taxicab, saw that the trunks were tied with string onto the grid at the back which weight gave the impression that the front wheels of the car were about to lift off. After a great deal of altercation the men got the hat-box, which was light in weight but enormous in size and had already caused trouble innumerable times on my African stops, (I had been told to bring at least half-a-dozen garden party hats) secured onto the roof. Dost Mohammed himself perched on top of my bedding roll beside the driver, blocking my view to the front which was just as well as the Sikh driver drove like Jehu hunched over the wheel, with one hand permanently honking the horn at his side. When he changed gear, the steering wheel was left to its own devices for breath-taking seconds on end. I concentrated on looking out of the back window to see what damage we were leaving

3

in our trail. Amazingly there seemed to be no bodies, no massacre of the hordes of pedestrians missed by inches as they strolled across roads as if there was nothing in the way.

Our taxi scraped at speed past decrepit cars, bicycles by the dozen, lop-sided buses and fleets of *tongas* - small two-wheeled traps pulled by skinny ponies. A hand-cart spilled oranges and melons over the road in front of us but still we did not stop. Instead we swerved violently to half dislodge the hat-box which appeared in view outside the window. No question of stopping though. At last, and much to my relief, the taxi screeched to a halt in a narrow back street in front of the steps of a monumental-looking building, part Gothic, part Victorian architecture. Its five turreted stories rose to a great dome in the centre.

In those days the unverified story ran rife that the architect had made a terrible bloomer. When he came to investigate the building he found that the ornate frontage he had designed to face the sea front, instead was facing this mean little street. So ashamed was he (so the story ran) that he committed suicide. There is no doubt that where I stood looked to me like a grand entrance, but then when later I walked round to the front I thought that looked grandiose enough as well.

But now as Dost Mohammed supervised the unloading of my hand luggage, an aghast thought struck me. What would they charge in a place like this? I would be bankrupt before I got to the station.

'Taj Mahal very good hotel for Miss-sahib to spend day,' I heard the bearer pronouncing after he had instructed the hotel porter to take charge of my suitcase and bedding-roll.

'But...but,' I stammered, 'it's rather too... Cannot we go straight to the station?'

'Colonel Resident-sahib pay,' Dost Mohammed clicked as if he could read my thoughts while flourishing a wallet taken from the folds of his *achkan*. 'Station no good for Miss-sahibs to wait; *badmashes* watch on station.' I was soon to discover that these 'bad men' frequently came into the bearer's conversation, particularly where Miss-sahibs were concerned. He turned away abruptly from me and began a slanging match with the Sikh driver over the exorbitant extra fare he was apparently asking for all the luggage. It was obvious even to my newcomer's eyes that my proud escort from the north thoroughly despised the southern scum of Bombay, also that the driver knew he had not a hope of squeezing a pice more out of Dost Mohammed than was his due anymore than the porters had. Nevertheless the driver was having a very good try by the sound of his voice.

The thought of the beggars I had been besieged by on arrival worried me, and on the steps of the hotel I asked the bearer about them. 'How do they live? Where do they sleep?' I wanted to know.

'It is profession. None starve. All have some roof over head.' I learned later that many of the beggars were purposely maimed at birth for the lucrative

4

living of their touts, and that Bombay in the thriving '30s of my arrival prided itself that few slept out on pavements as is the case today. As I stepped through the portals of the Taj Mahal, I found the hotel was as magnificent inside as it was out. An arcaded corridor, flanked by expensive looking shops and a hair and beauty salon, led to an ornate reception desk. I was expected. A room had been booked for the day. I had never heard of such a thing before. Surely one could rest in the lounge? The old fashioned lift of open wrought-iron splendour sedately carried me up between an ornate balustraded staircase to the third floor where I was led to an enormous double suite complete with its marble-floored bathroom almost as large again.

'Miss-sahib stay here all day,' Dost Mohammed instructed. 'Not to leave hotel,' he waggled a bony finger at me. 'I come fetch after dinner-*khana*. Now I take big luggage to register through journey.'

I went over to the window and looked out onto the Gateway of India built to commemorate the visit of King George V and Queen Mary in 1911. The Gateway looked to me like a rather wider Arc de Triomphe but one that led nowhere. The inside and surroundings were kept clear of debris and bird droppings by sweepers. The inevitable beggars were barred from the arch by a blue-uniformed policeman on duty. Before the Gateway, steps led down to where boats with awnings vied with one another in offering trips to see the famed cave carvings on Elephanta Island in the harbour. In the distant haze could be glimpsed the hills on the rocky Deccan coast, and in the bay sea-going craft were heading towards the Seven Islands in preparation for their return - now it was late September - across the Arabian Sea to Mombasa from whence I had just come. I had watched these beautiful long-prowed dhows with their lofty sails and cargoes of fruit and ivory, in African waters. From there they had caught the trade winds of May. Now I saw them ready to return with the wind laden with cotton, tea, spices and silks.

༄ ༄ ༄ ༄

After taking a bath I was dozing on the bed in the cool of my luxurious suite, half closed eyes mesmerized by the big electric fan gently gyrating overhead in the lofty ceiling, when there was a telephone call from a couple I knew on the *Tairea* who suggested they take me out that afternoon.

'But Dost Mohammed said I must stay put.' I hesitated.

'You don't have to take any notice of what your bearer says,' they laughed. 'Come on. We'll go out for a swim at Breach Candy and then take you to early dinner at the Yacht Club, the most exclusive Club in India. There'll be plenty of time for you to catch the train after that. Half the *Tairea* will be on it.'

And so we did but not before I had visited the beauty salon below to have a mud-pack facial in an attempt to restore my damp looks before being whisked

5

The Gateway of India, Bombay

The Taj Mahal Hotel, Bombay

6

away in a smart car by my friends. The husband was a '*box-wallah*', a businessman dressed for the Club in a white suit with white lace-up shoes. I was rather on tenterhooks as to Dost Mohammed's reaction should he come to my room and find me not there, but in the event he was waiting for me downstairs when I returned. When he saw I had been with 'sahibs', he seemed not too put out.

Outside after that day of swimming and fun, the heat hung heavy, breathless with dust, though degrees cooler than under the intense blaze of the sun. The night hid the squalor I had seen earlier in the day with roads lined with shacks and tin-roofed stalls, the smell of Bombay's drains and marsh-land permeating the air. In contrast the Marine Drive, now prettily necklaced with lights and smelling of spiced salt breezes, reminded me of a Mediterranean promenade on a hot summer's night.

The Victoria railway terminus, another enormous structure as lofty as a cathedral, was even more crowded than the port had been. Apparently, and for very low fares, thousands of people travelled every day by the slow trains which catered to carry as many as could cram themselves in. These people of all ages, groups and castes, made the platforms their homes for sometimes days on end until the right train arrived to carry them away. They waited patiently in family groups who sat round small charcoal braziers to cook their chappatis. They suckled their babies and, shrouded in sheets, curled up and slept on mats. They seemed to be able to sleep anywhere however uncomfortable the perch, and however noisy their surroundings. Goats, chickens and emaciated pi-dogs tumbled around by bare-bottomed toddlers with huge black eyes and snotty noses. Ancient crones were helped to their feet by stalwart sons and grandsons, and if too ill or weak to walk, were carried pick-a-back to the train followed by wives and children. I was struck by the thought that here in the stark poverty of their masses, no one was alone.

Well, neither was *I* anymore! I took my cue from the Indian women and followed closely behind Dost Mohammed's tall back as he shouldered a passage ahead through and round the reclining crowds.

We stopped by the train. 'You have a family?' I gesticulated to a group.

'*Han* Miss-sahib, I have big family, many, many sons!'

'These people seem ill,' I exclaimed above the concertinaed banging of the long train as carriages were added. I had skidded on what looked like blood; and I had seen blood on men's lips.

'It is the *paan*! See, the betel nut they chew between the leaf. Then they spit,' Dost Mohammed shook his head at my ignorance. I could almost hear him tuttutting. Yet I fancied I detected a trace of a chuckle. 'Stay here Miss-sahib,' he ordered in his manner. 'I find reserved carriage; then I see to luggage. These fools cannot be trusted.'

2
Journey to Kashmir

In the train I shared a brand new, shiny, blue, air conditioned compartment for 'Ladies Only'. The two bunks were made up for the night. The other occupant, already installed with bundles of luggage, was a very pregnant Indian girl. Her Western-suited husband hovered outside on the platform.

'Will you be so kind as to please keep an eye on my wife?' the man implored in a public school accent. 'We travel to family home in Delhi for arrival of our first *baccha*. I am a few carriages down the train should you wish to call me.'

This did not seem very promising there being no corridors on the train. 'Don't worry,' I said with an assurance I did not feel, 'I'll take care of her.'

'Thank you; thank you. Very, very kind...'

Whistles blew. Smoke trailed past the carriage window as we slid out of Victoria Station. I looked doubtfully at the girl sitting silently beside me in the coupé. From the superiority of my twenty-one years she looked to me a mere child though I supposed she must have been nearly fifteen, for marriage below the age of fourteen was against the law. As round as she was tall, her slippered feet scarcely touched the floor. She was dressed in a pink-patterned shimmering sari, and her black hair was severely tied back into a long thick oiled plait reaching to well below where her waist should have been. She seemed very shy and did not speak English as fluently as her husband. In fact I imagined I was the first English woman she had met. We were both obviously tired, and we soon settled down to sleep after only exchanging a few polite words.

In the middle of the night, I awoke on my top bunk to hear, to my horror, groans. 'Are you all right?' I asked leaning over the side.

'Baba comes,' she said wild-eyed, and let forth a shout. In the dim blue light above my bunk I made a mental note of the communication cord's position. After a bit of listening I decided to get dressed. There would be no more sleep that night. I climbed down to sit beside her.

I do not know which one of us was the more terrified. She might well have seen childbirth before in the *bibighar* women's quarters of her home. Perhaps in her fear of knowing what was coming she made a point of groaning in anticipation right from the start. It was not long, though, before she was screaming lustily with all her lungs every time a pain started. She made not the slightest attempt to stifle the sound and endure. I knew nothing about nursing or babies being born but I knew I was squeamish to a degree and that there would be blood about. I did know that the umbilical cord had to be cut. What with? My nail scissors in my make-up case? In those days the details of birth were not talked about in laymen's circles, and ignorant as I was on the subject, I found the girl's screams unnerving to say the least. I wished she would shut up. I became more and more cross. I was sure she did not have to make all that indulgent noise. After enduring for a while, I burst out to tell her in no uncertain terms to keep her breath for the birth; but it made no difference. She continued to yell at each pain.

Between these she appeared quite composed and told me in halting English of her sheltered upbringing, her arranged marriage, and how she had not seen her husband until her wedding day. He was kind, she said, though she did not care for her mother-in-law who would now take over completely and boss her around. She prayed, she said, for a son in this the greatest moment of her life - the birth of her first-born.

'But, please, not in the train,' I urged, the agitation showing in my voice, 'please, *please* not in the carriage. Can't you hold it back or something?' She began to yell again. She threw herself around on the bunk to such an extent I was afraid she would hurt herself and damage the baby.

'For God's sake stop screaming,' I snapped. 'If you don't I'll slap your face.'

She did stop a bit then which proved my point, though I felt like a criminal when she looked at me hurtfully with her beautiful heavily outlined doe eyes.

The periods between pains grew shorter, and still the train rumbled on with no stops. I decided that when things became acute I'd pull the communication cord and risk having to pay the fifty rupee fine as inscribed above the chain. (Five pounds was a lot of money in those days). Perhaps Dost Mohammed would take the sum out of the Resident's purse as being part of the hazards of a journey in India? Anyway what good would pulling the communication cord do if it stopped the train in the middle of nowhere? I peered through the slats and saw only blackness. It was unlikely that there would be a doctor on the train, and the girl's anxious husband would probably be just as useless as I. Whatever happened, I vowed I would take a crash course in midwifery before ever travelling again in a Ladies Coupé in India!

I decided to hang on; I remembered a girl at school saying first babies took days and days of rolling about in agony. It had sounded so awful to me, and now was *proving* to be so awful, that I was sure I would never be brave enough to have a baby myself. I would have to tell my intended - whomever he might be - that if this was what he wanted me to endure he had chosen the wrong woman....

In an endeavour to show kindness I held the girl's hands and rubbed her back when she was quiet, and it did seem to me that her screams were less loud which put me in a fresh panic less she was becoming exhausted and I would have a corpse on my hands. So it was with enormous relief that what seemed like hours later I felt a jolt followed by the screech of brakes being applied with the lurch

9

of the train as we drew into a station. This baby was, thank God, not going to be born in the train, but neither was it going to be born in Delhi. With her husband supporting her, half carrying her, I watched the pair disappearing into the crowd to produce one more baby to add to all those millions. Momentarily I felt sad to have lost her. I had come to know her intimately, and seen for the first time the trauma of pre-birth - yet I did not even know her name.

It was an experience I never forgot. I hope she had a son.

꽃   꽃   꽃   꽃

At Delhi the air-conditioned carriage went no further. Dost Mohammed settled me into an ordinary coupé reserved for ladies which I had to myself with its own tiny wash basin and lavatory off. The carriage had been waiting to be coupled onto the train in a siding in the sun and was boiling hot. With much shouting and gesticulating under Dost Mohammed's exacting eye, coolies placed a large slab of ice in a flatish tin on the floor.

To begin with, under a whirring fan, this did produce a freshness in the carriage. Then the ice began to melt, and when the train started up again and set off puffing clouds of smoke on its way, the water sloshed from side to side with the rocking of the train as it gathered speed, and more and more of the ice melted until the compartment floor became a small lake and I had to sit with my feet up on the berth. To add to the heat and the discomfort of trying to avoid the wet floor, in a very short time everything, including me, became covered with a fine film of red dust. This old first class carriage I was in could not have been more of a contrast from the pristine newness of my erstwhile air-conditioned shiny blue one.

At nightfall a coolie came in to mop up the floor after which Dost Mohammed opened my bedding-roll (which had been bought at the Army & Navy Store in London and already used in Kenya), and made up my bed on the bunk with the mattress, sheets, and pillow therein. Then Dost Mohammed proceeded to shut and lock on the inside the mosquito-proof wire netting, and the wooden slatted window. The glass windows were presumably only for winter. 'Please leave the slatted window open,' I protested at the exclusion of air and light.'

'Miss-sahib keep window shut all night,' the bearer admonished severely as I might have guessed he would.

'Why, Dost Mohammed?' I voiced tentatively. *My* wishes did not seem to come into anything with him!

'Bad men slash fly-proof windows easy. Plenty of *thuggees* come along train roof. They dacoits; they climb in and steal. They kill many peoples by cloth strangling, silent and swift,' he made a graphic garrotting motion to illustrate. 'These *badmashes* watch out for Miss-sahibs travelling!'

10

For the second night running I barely slept. At any moment I expected to see a shadowy figure forcing open the slats on murderous intent. This time I would well and truly pull the communication cord, that is if there was time before... At least they said Indians did not rape Miss-sahibs. They only kidnapped them and held them to ransom, I tried to comfort myself.

When at last daylight filtered through the slats and I felt it safe to open the window, I found the air outside cooler. The view was one of rolling countryside, little mud villages tucked into the folds with many people already out working in the fields. The train stopped in this cultivated country to allow hundreds of Indians to disgorge from the crowded carriages. Openly they squatted down in rows along the embankments to relieve themselves after the night's journey.

I was amazed how Dost Mohammed remained so clean-looking under the conditions he travelled in, in the packed servants' carriage further down the train. For luggage, beside a modest bedding roll, he carried only a white bundle. At one station I saw him undo it on the platform and take out a tin bowl. Surreptitiously I watched from my window as he removed his *pugri* to reveal close-cut grizzled hair. He looked so different without his *pugri* on that had I not been watching him I could not have picked him out of the crowd.

I went on looking to see what he would do next. He proceeded to wash his hands and feet thoroughly under a pump tap. He then, with much sloshing and spitting of water, cleansed his teeth with his fingers. A *nai* (barber) appeared at his command to shave him with a cut-throat razor. Both men settled down to squat before one another on the platform as indifferently as if they were in a saloon. The barber pinned Dost Mohammed's characteristic moustaches out of the way and proceeded to get down to work with his lethal instrument, just finishing in time to allow the bearer to leap onto his already moving carriage. I must admit that I was on tenterhooks by then lest my guide and protector should not make the dash in time and I lose him.

At Rawalpindi, near the borders of the North West Frontier Province and Kashmir, the Resident's orderly-chauffeur, Hassan-ud-Din was waiting for us. With smiles the men greeted one another, and then the driver stood stiffly to attention to salute me, his hand against the red and gold ribbon in his khaki *pugri*. I felt like a thousand dollars!

With the two sitting in front of the black Vauxhall Saloon, a flag encased on the bonnet (it was only unfurled if the Resident was in the car), I sat grandly back in the rear and wished some of the girls at St James's Secretarial College could see me now. As far as I knew not even those who had passed out top - I had not, book-keeping having defeated me - had such an exalted and fascinating job as I had landed, and in one of the great beauty spots of the world. Relieved to have the train journey safely behind me, I was enormously excited by the next step and avidly looked about me.

The bare plains of the cantonment town of Rawalpindi gave way to undulations as we entered foothills. The westering sun glinted with sparking

11

flashes on fine grains of mica in the soil on the verges. The road curled and turned with sharp rises through spruce and pine forests up into the hill-station of Murree, 7,500 feet above sea level where the air was blessedly cool in the lengthening shadows.

I spent the night in a comfortable though ramshackle corrugated-iron-roofed hotel perched on the edge of a ridge with views looking over a steep *khud*. I slept deeply in the quietness of those thickly wooded glorious hills, my windows thrown open to the resinous scent of firs mingling with that of sweet heliotrope in the beds beneath my window. I dreamed that night of friendly ghosts of the past who had stayed there, all those brave Victorian *memsahibs* and their babies and *ayahs* who had endured the lengthy journey by horse-drawn carriages to be with their menfolk serving on the Frontier. Peaceful Murree too had had its troubles in those far off days, when it had been attacked and fought over by *badmashes* from the hill tribes during the Mutiny.

❦ ❦ ❦ ❦

Promptly at eight o'clock next morning we started off on the near two hundred miles to Srinagar. The rough road at first descended. It swirled dust, scattered loose gravel, and twisted and turned its tortuous way for mile after mile in deep valleys which followed the rushing Jhelum river. Steep brown hills hemmed us in. Once again it was oppressively hot.

Every so often we stopped for a wash and refreshment at wayside *Dak* or Post bungalows, some of them Government rest houses. The bungalows had been built in the previous centuries every fifteen miles or so for travellers and the change of their horses. Originally they were used as centres where the *dak* - the mail - was delivered and collected. For these stops I was profoundly grateful. I would have died rather than ask the inscrutable Dost Mohammed or the impressive Hassan-ud-Din to stop to allow me to squat behind some inadequate cover on the wayside of sparse straggly bushes. Even in England one did not mention to a male that one needed to 'disappear' for the embarrassment it would bring to both.

Gradually the valley widened to give way to a gently rolling plain of fertile farmland framed by hills and mountains. We passed a village and stopped by a wooden bridge where I got out to stretch my legs. At last here I was on the threshold of my goal of the enchanted Vale of Kashmir.

Wildly excited I breathed in great gulps of pure air which freshness made me feel slightly drunk together with the stunning beauty of my surroundings. At an altitude of 5,500 feet above the hot plains of India, I had reached a new world, the world of Shangri-la, one of 'emeralds and rubies set in pearls'. I walked a little way beyond the bridge and found myself standing in the midst of fields, indeed the colour of emeralds, some filled with patches of ruby poppies. Other fields

12

The enchanted Vale of Kashmir

were of golden mustard, others still of blue linseed, all interspersed by lakes sparkling like diamonds. This 'jewel', so described by the Mughal emperors, was set in a series of eternally snow-capped 'pearls' of the huge mountains of the Himalayan and Karakoram Ranges. It was the most beautiful sight I had ever seen with its waving green fields, brilliant diamond water, mountain summits topped by everlasting snows reaching deep blue sky. Though it was September as yet the leaves on the trees had scarcely begun to turn. Truly I thought with the Mughal Emperor of old:

> 'If there be a Paradise on the face of the earth,
> It is here, it is here, it is here!'

Hassan-ud-Din drove on very fast down a long, completely straight road lined with sentinel poplar trees. He scarcely slowed up through villages, horn blaring, chickens scattering, grubby children wearing colourful caps waving as they recognized the car with furled flag. Enchanted, I waved back. Hassan-ud-Din did not slow up until we came to the narrow bazaar streets of Srinagar, summer capital of Kashmir, where thin white cows wandered unperturbed and safe through the traffic. Sometimes they sat immovable in the middle of the road chewing the cud despite horns blaring from every direction. I saw mangy pariah dogs pushing their noses into mounds of refuse, their backbones sticking out like skeletons, and I thought this is Bombay over again, this is poverty, this is India whether south, west, east or north.

We came to a Lodge where a sentry stood to attention outside his box as the car swept through the open gates and up a short drive to come to rest before the stone steps of the rambling, half-timbered Kashmir Residency. On the balustraded steps stood a colourful *chaprassi* smart in a long scarlet *achkan* coat with a gold braided breastplate, a broad cummerbund around his ample stomach. A man long in the service of the Raj, he made a striking figure with his white beard and moustaches tucked into his fine Sikh's turban.

The *chaprassi* opened the car door. As I got out I glanced up at the two-storied mansion that was to be my abode. The building was covered with creepers hanging down over an arcaded porch and hiding much of the brick-work interspersed with beams of wood criss-crossed up to the gabled roof. Covered balconies on ground and first floors ran right round the sides and back. I was astonished. Up here in far Kashmir, in this alien setting of vast lakes and towering mountains, the Residency basked serenely in the westering sun. It looked to me just like a large English country house set in an English garden of spacious soft green lawns, shady trees, and colourful herbaceous borders. Had it not been for the *chaprassis* in their uniforms, the Sikh driver, and....

I turned to look for Dost Mohammed to thank him for looking after me on the journey, but he had gone. Discreetly and silently he had faded away now his task was accomplished.

14

The rambling half-timbered Kashmir Residency

Although I often met him about the house in the times to come, his face remained inscrutable, a lofty salaam the only answer to my friendly smile with no sign that for thousands of miles he had guarded me and shepherded me under his ever watchful eye even to escorting me at a stop along the platform to the restaurant car for a meal, and then coming to fetch me at a further station to take me back to my carriage. Now he was no longer 'mine'; now once again he was exclusively the Lady-sahib's shadow, forestalling her every wish, carrying her trays to her room when she was indisposed, guarding *her* with his life.

I will admit to feeling a twinge of jealousy!

3
The Kashmir Residency

When there were no house guests, we four had breakfast at a round table in the bay window of the dining-room overlooking the drive and garden. On the expanse of green lawn facing us towered four huge chenar trees said to be three centuries old; their leaves were just beginning to turn colour.

The 'we' consisted of the Resident, Lieutenant Colonel Denholm Fraser (later he was knighted), a wiry energetic man in grey flannel trousers, yellow and maroon Central India Horse tie, and ancient tweed jacket. 'Dem', as he was habitually known, looked amazingly boyish for his fifty years despite peppered military moustache and greying hair.

Dem's wife, Sheila, had put on weight since the birth of three sons in rapid succession, but her complexion was still like a girl's. Her features were classical with oval face, Grecian nose and full lips. Her long glinting wavy brown hair was worn 'up' twisted into a chignon. It was the delight of Dem who would never let her cut it, not even in the hot weather when it became a torment. She was a woman who followed fashion and liked to dress in pretty pastel shades. Her slender legs were clad in silk stockings, dainty feet encased in high-heeled open-work shoes.

Though she always appeared groomed, she could contrast the smart look of red lips, eye shadow and mascara, by dressing in winter in brogues and a kilt, slacks and shirts in summer. Having spent much of her childhood in India - her father was in the Indian Medical Service - she was from an early age a first class shot and fisherwoman. Whatever she was doing, whether gardening or 'ghooming' in the jungle, she always looked immaculate. Even when languishing in bed (and as so many women did, she suffered much ill health in India), with one thick plait draped over a shoulder and no make-up on, she still looked beautiful. Besides this she was talented and intelligent. Anything she took up she did well. Had she lived in the present generation when women of her calibre had careers, she would have started up some kind of fashion boutique, hat shop, art gallery or flower arranging business. As things stood she was a great asset to her husband in his career, and an expert in economizing, for neither of them having private means, and despite the luxurious way of living, mainly government funded, they were perpetually 'short'.

The third member of the household breakfasting at the round table on that morning, was 'Ronnie' Wood, a masculine-looking woman in corduroy trousers, shirt and tie, lock of hair falling over forehead. She had pale, protruding, heavily lidded eyes, a toothy smile and a cigarette perpetually dangling from the

Dem Fraser, the Resident, with Sheila his wife (née Battye)

corner of her lips. She had left her kennels in England in competent hands to come out to India for a spell to breed from the two valuable golden retrievers she had earlier handed over to the Frasers. The intention was to sell any puppies produced to local dignitaries and rajas which exercise would not only give everyone concerned pleasure but would help to pay for the boys' schooling. On that first morning I was told that Glory, the platinum coloured bitch, was soon to have her first litter by Roy of a darker more reddy shade of coat. The dogs lay under the breakfast table, Glory's head resting lovingly on Sheila's feet.

As for myself I felt privileged to be the fourth member of this distinguished group. Relieved to have arrived all in one piece in a place that was even more thought-inspiring than I had anticipated, I was very much on my best behaviour and also a little apprehensive lest I didn't pass muster. Unattached since the grandmother who had brought me up in France had died, the question I asked myself was would I make the grade in this sophisticated *milieu* of 'high-ups' as they were known in India?

I was aware that PAs were required to be *capable de tout*. I thought I was fairly capable having run my grandmother's affairs in her last years, but *'de tout'* when I had dismally failed the book-keeping and had stuck at a 100 wpm shorthand instead of achieving the required 120? I was fluent in French but of what use was that out here? I had been told that I must learn to speak Urdu. A *munshi* was arriving that very day to start my lessons which, with the weather still fine would take place under one of the chenar trees. Why was Urdu so important, I had asked. I thought Indians spoke English? By no means, I was told. Most did not. There were some two hundred different languages in India, Gujerati in the south for one, Pashtu on the North West Frontier and so on, but, unless in remote areas, they all spoke Urdu which I needed to know so that I could communicate with the servants in their own tongue.

Yet the two most important retainers in the household spoke English. One of them was waiting on us at the breakfast table. He was de Mello, a Christian, the middle-aged, bare-headed Goan butler, small and efficient, a rotund man in starched white jacket and trousers, his plimsoles, on sockless brown feet, heavily blancoed. (I had noticed that all the other servants I had seen indoors including Dost Mohammed, went bare-footed). De Mello was the major-domo of the establishment, who together with his friend, de Souza, the Mugh cook from Chittagong, Bengal, had been with Dem and Sheila for many years and who in tandem were responsible for the smooth running of the household.

Now, in this Residency, where the Resident lived in palatial style with a staff to match an ambassador's, I gathered de Souza was excelling himself in inventing delectable dishes for the endless stream to be fed.

De Mello was responsible for hiring and training local staff for the lesser jobs and making sure there were no *badmashes* among the *chowkidars*, the night watchmen, though all Kashmiris were considered to be rogues, and the most attractive ones at that with their dark-eyed good looks. De Souza's greatest test was soon to come with the advent of the Viceregal party for the famous autumn shoot, said to be the most fabulous one in the whole of India. I listened with awe to the complexities of this visit of a family of giants which seemed to so exercise the Frasers. I supposed that as the representative of the King Emperor, it must be rather like George VI inviting himself to stay in one's humble home. I was pondering on this when the conversation turned to family matters.

'War breaking out in Europe is going to cause us problems,' Dem mused. 'We'll soon run out of places for them to stay in the holidays. The grandparents are really too old to cope any more with three energetic boys.'

'They must come out to India,' took up Sheila emphatically, 'and soon, while passages can still be booked. It's already getting difficult.'

'Certainly not,' Dem came down sternly. 'What sort of education would they get here? They'll end up speaking chee-chee; I won't *hear* of it.'

'You shouldn't have brought me out,' laughed Ronnie lighting up another cigarette. I gathered from that remark that she had previously looked after the boys in the holidays.

Sheila did not reply to her husband's dampener to her wish. It would be interesting, I thought, summing both parents up, to see who would win this obvious battle of wills. I already had a shrewd idea who would, by a mixture of charm and subtlety. Sheila was far too clever a woman to use nagging tactics or even tears. No, it would be a gentle wearing-down process. I'd lay a bet that in the end Dem would give way!

✿ ✿ ✿ ✿

After breakfast Dem conducted me to his dark half-panelled study at the back of the house. It had an ornately carved fireplace, on either side of which were massive integral bookcases stuffed with volumes. Above the mantelpiece lintel hung a string of photographs in black frames. These were of successive Residents dating back to the time in the last century when the British sold to Raja Gulab Singh of Jammu the mountainous regions of Kashmir for a *crore* of rupees: three-quarters of a million pounds sterling.

Dem showed me my adjoining study as large as his again and just as dark. The room was complete with desk and prominent typewriter. That was fine as long as I was not required to keep the books as well.

'Your work with me will be light,' Dem informed, 'unless, of course, there is a crisis when all hell will be let loose between the factions.'

'Crisis?' I echoed alarmed. 'I thought all was peaceful here?'

'The situation is ripe for possible subversion. There is always tension in Kashmir. I'll explain in a minute. As I was saying, your work for me will normally be light. I will require you from time to time to take down certain

20

The study at the back of the Residency

confidential documents and letters which we do not want to go through the *babus* in the offices of the Secretariat.'

'What sort of "confidential"?'

'Defence; emergency plans in case of trouble - that kind of thing. The threat here is a clash between the ruling Hindus - Dogras from Jammu State - and the mass of people who resent being ruled by them. Same thing happens in reverse in Hyderabad State only not so volatile there where a Muslim is hereditary ruler over a mass of Hindus. There are also private letters to be typed to HH, His Highness, as we call the Maharaja. He dislikes the British; is suspicious of our every move; has to be handled extremely delicately.'

Dem led the way back to his study, indicated I sit down in a comfortable leather chair, offered me a cigarette from a carved walnut box, at which I shook my head. Occasionally I indulged in a Balkan Sobranie after dinner for the scent of it. Though I had tried to smoke to be like everyone else of my generation, I could never take to it. Dem himself lit up a cigarette which he held in a holder. He proceeded to put me in the picture about the Government of India and Kashmir in particular. I knew only the bare outlines. He was a good talker on a subject none knew better than he. I listened attentively.

'My job here is more diplomatic than administrative,' he started off, 'Kashmir is an Independent State as you know. The Princes, over six hundred and seventy of them, rule one-third of the subcontinent; the rest is British India ruled from Delhi. There are fifty of us Politicals, all hand picked by the Viceroy!' Dem gave me his boyish grin. 'We advise the Independent Princes. There are only two thousand British in the ICS, the Indian Civil Service. Indians are being trained and promoted into the jobs for when the change-over comes. If justice prevails and bloodshed is to be avoided India *must* remain one country.'

'How soon do you expect the hand-over to come?' I asked. The way he spoke made it look as if I'd be packed off back to England within only a few months of my arrival.

'It *was* to have been in two or three years time. Now they'll have to wait until the war is won. I expect our troops will be sent over the water, the forbidden *Kala Pani* or Black Water, to the Western Front as happened in the last war. The troops have to say *pujas* to be purified from the defilement on their return. Same old story twenty years on, pitchforked into the cold and the trenches with high casualties, and here we are again hopelessly prepared. The Indian Army will once more do its stuff magnificently. But back to the lesson. That phrase "Divide and Rule", used by those who don't know, is utter rot for this century - a relic of John Company days when there was some truth in it. We have an amazing system of justice in British India when you consider the millions to watch over. Even the humblest and poorest of "untouchables" can have their say before their District Magistrate, the key man out here sent young and inexperienced to administer enormous areas of *mofussil* country. He learns quickly how to judge the complex

22

cases of land claims, murders when a body is found down a well, and all the family disputes. The first thing the District Magistrate has to do is to learn the language - same as you have to -' Dem gave me his cheerful grin, 'so that he can understand and speak fluently to the elders who come to state their cases in the *jirga* law courts held in the open in the villages. It works brilliantly. British justice is accepted as fair by all, even by the criminal *thuggees.*'

'I've heard that word before: they're out to murder Miss-sahibs!'

'Oh. Heard from Dost Mohammed? Yes, he would. Our greatest headache at the moment is not *thuggees* but Congress. Ruddy politicians in white Gandhi caps putting a spoke in our plan of handing over a smoothly running affair. If we bow to pressure in too much of a hurry before the new government has established its control, there will be spontaneous bloodshed between the sects. We have proved time and again they can live side by side in peace if the government is seen to be fair and unbiased. We pin our hopes on Jinnah, a great man though unfortunately an ailing one. A devout Muslim he is as firmly against partition of the country as we are. Our aim is one huge Independent India, the greatest democratic power in the East, one that can stand up to any Communist threat. But enough of my hobby-horse...'

'You were going to tell me about the here and now.'

'Quite. To continue with the lecture, we have three Residencies in all: Sialkot in the Plains for the winter months; high up in Gulmarg in the summer; here in between. Our "beat" extends over huge isolated mountainous districts known as the Gilgit Agency. Those are the Hunza and Nagar feudal States which are administered by our Political Agent, known as the PA - not to be mistaken for you!' Dem said with a twinkle, 'Our present APA happens to be Sheila's eldest brother. He'll be coming down to report. It takes a week's trek to get here from Gilgit by the most precipitous tracks and flimsy bridges imaginable over torrential ravines. Have you a head for heights?'

'I don't really know; I've never...'

'Well you'd better have! You'll be required to go next year.' Dem barely stopped in his flow of words. 'One can fly these days. Sheila and I did a trip up this summer. Amazing. *Between* mountain peaks. The tiny plane which has to be small enough to land on Gilgit's hazardous airstrip, can't fly high enough to get over the mountain tops! Given the time I prefer to trek.'

'Now to Princes. Each has an allotment of gun salutes by which they set much store to distinguish the greater from the lesser. Kashmir is one of the topmost States with a twenty-one salute although we are only registered as a second-class Residency. Other States have from thirteen guns upwards, less if you are only a Raja. If the Prince pleases or displeases, the Viceroy can add or subtract a couple of guns. Great kudos is set by this ritual. For instance the smaller Princes have to meet a visiting Viceroy on the borders of their States, while His Highness the Maharaja of Kashmir only has to go as far as his drawing-room door! Our HH (Maharaja stands for 'Great King') enjoys enormous wealth and rank.'

'If he is so rich why doesn't he do more for his subjects? Driving through the bazaar yesterday... well... is it true that the Kashmiri is the poorest of the poor?'

'I'm afraid so. The standard of living here is very low. With the lakes and steep mountain sides the people have little land on which to cultivate crops, and to own land is what counts to an Indian. However, let me say here and now that, compared to some others, our Hari Singh is a most excellent and compassionate ruler,' Dem replied loyal to HH. 'One good point is that taxes here are less than in British India. HH holds powers of life and death over his subjects and is above the law himself. For instance you can be imprisoned for life for killing a cow. With so many Brahmins and high caste Dogras in Kashmir the sanctity of the cow is paramount. As you no doubt observed on your drive here, it is the easiest thing to run into a half-starved beast wandering the roads. Hence we do not allow our officials to drive. Have to wait till we get to Sialkot in British India to keep our hands in. It would be awkward to say the least if the Resident or his wife killed a cow and got locked up in Akbar's Fort on the hill! Then too it is an offence to import beef in any form. My father was Resident here before the last war.'

I nodded. I had met Sir Stuart Fraser in England, a marvellous old man who lived to be in his hundredth year looked after by his unmarried daughter Vi. I knew that he had been a great friend of the old Maharaja, Sir Pertab Singh, the present Maharaja's uncle, and that Dem as a child was out here before he was sent to preparatory school in England. He had ridden and played cricket with the then Prince, his contemporary in age, young Hari Singh.

'Hari Singh and I were good friends,' Dem went on, 'and still get on well which is more than can be said of one with whom HH was daggers drawn. Funny chap, that Resident. Left his wife and ran off to Kenya with his secretary, so watch out! As I was saying, my father used to recount the story of how his Political Agent was taken to court for ordering meat-extract out from England for his invalid wife, and how the then Residency Surgeon was closely questioned on his children's jar of bulls-eye sweets! HH has absolute power over any internal matter, but he is not permitted to deal direct with other States, nor any foreign power. Moreover if a Prince grossly misrules, the Viceroy has the right to banish him. We also administer in the case of a minor on the *gadi* - throne - as my father did in the State of Kolhapur. Yet whatever the Prince does in the privacy of his own royal circle in his palaces, however much against British laws or however depraved, he is seldom suspended.'

'Who really rules then?' I asked, reeling from all this information.

'HH does. But if you ask who has the ultimate power? *We* do! The fact is that practically all the Princes want the British to stay. They know only too well that under an Indian Government they will lose their private wealth and

24

moreover lose the special privileges we have built up for them in return for their loyalty.'

'I remember hearing talk about a scandal that happened in England before I was born. The Mr 'A' case. It was about this Maharaja wasn't it?'

'It was. That was a bad business. HH was a young man, a greenhorn and on his first trip to Europe in pursuit of his education. It is no wonder he has been distrustful of the British ever since. Here,' Dem said rummaging through a drawer in his desk and handing me a file, 'you'd better start by looking through this.'

I took it to my study and began to read:

༷ ༷ ༷ ༷

'THE BLACKMAIL CASE INVOLVING THE MAHARAJAH OF KASHMIR

When the First World War ended, Hari Singh, heir to his uncle's throne, was sent off to Europe on a grand tour to complete his education as a prime Indian Prince.

A certain Captain Charles Arthur, a British Officer convalescing in Kashmir, somehow wheedled himself into the royal household and into the affections of the young Prince who made him sole aide-de-camp for the tour. The then present Resident in Kashmir, not thinking highly of Captain Arthur's record, objected, but the Prince insisted. The Viceroy was approached and agreed to the appointment. The result was disastrous.

Hari Singh, an innocent and kind young man, was carried away by the heady atmosphere in Europe. He fell easily into the trap set for him.

At an adjoining box at the Albert Hall for the Victory Parade Ball to celebrate the first anniversary of the Armistice, was planted the carefully selected blonde and vivacious Mrs Maude Robinson. Hari Singh, bejewelled, scented and impressionable, fell fatefully in love.

It seems that Maude was not a totally bad sort. She became very fond of her lover. They lived together in England and then went to Paris where Captain Arthur and his flunkeys arranged the final scene which included finding the absent Mr Robinson and bribing him to crash into the bedroom at the Hotel St James in the early hours of Boxing Day morning. Maude was so incensed that she attacked him, while the kind hearted Prince was reputed to have pulled her back saying, "After all, Maudie, he IS your husband."

The couple retired to the sanctuary of another hotel and sought the advice of the unsuspected Captain who pointed out that in view of the delicacy of the Prince's position as heir to his uncle - who apparently was not too fond of him - the only course was to purchase the husband's silence.

Then and there Hari Singh made out a cheque for £150,000 with a promise for a second one for the same amount in due course, enormous sums in those days.

Then came the ponderous and complicated business of the greedy Captain's double crossing of Mr Robinson and other accomplices. At last things began to go wrong for Captain Arthur. The Banks involved became suspicious; solicitors cried blackmail; Maudie Robinson suffered a nervous breakdown and the Prince returned disconsolate to Srinagar. He had lost a lot of money, and worse, he had lost his love whom he had hoped to make his concubine. Before the debacle she had agreed to come and live in Kashmir.

Eventually the case came up in the Law Courts with Lord Justice Darling, a noted wit, presiding. The public were riveted. The Secretary of State for India conveyed the need for absolute discretion and it was agreed the Prince would only be referred to as Mr 'A'. But it was too thin for disguise and when the news broke the British reaction in India was one of disgust that a young man entrusted to the care of an Englishman should have been misused in such a dastardly way. The guilty parties received prison sentences; the chapter was closed. "More sinned against than sinning" was the people's verdict.

Hari Singh soon after succeeded to the Kashmir throne. Now a bitter man, he never really trusted the British again.'

Phew! I thought, closing the file, and no wonder. And what a brilliant move of the powers that be to select Dem Fraser, a boyhood friend of the Maharaja's, for the post of Resident at this delicate and crucial time in the annals of the British in India.

Breakfasting in Residency garden

4

The Residency Garden

Known as *Platanus Orientalis* I now saw why the chenar of Kashmir in India was called a 'King among trees'. The foliage on these chenars dominating the Residency garden was so thick that sitting under them gave shade on the hottest day, and full protection from rain even in a downpour. Far above the topmost leaf could be seen the Takht-i-Suleiman, the throne of Solomon, a hill which appeared to rise its one thousand feet straight out of the water from the Srinagar plain. The small Hindu temple perched on its summit stood out whitely against the backcloth of a deep Kashmir-blue sky, crystal clear and unpolluted except for the rising wisps of wood fires burning far below.

The weedless lawn of the Residency had been tended, trimmed and watered over the decades by a flock of *malis* supervised by talented horticulturist English ladies who introduced new strains from the USA or Kew in England. The Residency garden had the reputation of being one of the most beautiful in the East in its superb setting with glimpses in spring between blossoming trees, of lakes and snow-covered mountains. This was undoubtedly true, but it was the Resident's wives, the Lady-sahibs, with their knowledge and their patient repeated instructions to the *malis*, *not* to plant in straight rows, who deserved the kudos for making it into a great garden. Many books were written about it; perhaps the best known the one with coloured illustrations by Colonel Younghusband, who himself was a one-time Resident as well as soldier and explorer.

Local water-colourists sat in the shade of the chenars to paint the delectable scene; many garden parties were held there and several wedding receptions for those lucky ones who knew the Resident and his lady well enough to ask for the privilege, and many were the Fêtes arranged to raise money for charity. These were always a great success, for everyone wanted to see beyond the lodges at either ends of the drive. It seemed that in this garden all fruit grew bigger, every plant grew taller and every flower larger than at home.

On my arrival there was a marvellous range of chrysanthemums with mammoth flowers of white, bronze and every shade of yellow to orange massing the beds edging the drive. Elsewhere round the garden bloomed a crop of magnificent roses. As well there were geraniums galore, scarlet salvias backed by pale pink semi-double begonias, Michaelmas daisies of pale mauve to deep purple hue, and flame gaillardias as tall as a man.

In the orchard, beyond what was known as 'The Cottage' - a small bungalow used as an extra guest house, for there were never enough rooms to accommodate all who wanted to stay - luscious apricots which we had for dessert were still ripening on the trees, as were the red Kashmir apples. The walnut trees were filled with fruit, delicious when eaten fresh. Soon these would be knocked down, the green peeled off, the nuts left to dry out in the sun until they became wrinkled. Nestling under the trees in the orchard was a carved wooden summer-house covered by a Fortune yellow rose in full bloom of golden sprays.

In their seasons all the English fruits reached plump and ripe perfection in this garden, all without the use of insecticides - still unknown out there. Wood ash was used to kill slugs; mustard and lime for other pests, soapy water for green-fly. But I always believed that apart from the climate of freezing winters enough to kill any dormant pests, and glorious sunny springs to ripen, the local manure which arrived in tons at the Residency *ghat* steps in boats was the secret. The manure was from the rotting vegetable patches on the man-made floating islands on the lakes in the Vale.

The soft fruits in the garden were painstakingly netted from the multitude of twittering birds who came back year after year to nest in the same spots. This always caused great excitement in the household: 'Our pair of flycatchers are back in their usual place by my bedroom window,' Sheila would announce delightedly. The birds came from their distant winterings to nest in the creepers on the house, in the bushes, in certain trees. I was told on my first day that the garden was at its best in spring after which it continued to be a mass of colour until late June when the heat became intense and the flowers began to wilt. I thought that it could not be more beautiful than it was on that autumn day of my arrival - but I was wrong.

❦   ❦   ❦   ❦

The profusion of species to pick gave endless scope for imaginative flower arrangements which took up a good part of my mornings. Sheila showed me how to arrange them à la Constance Spry before that august personage made the art popular, and before there was such helpful material as 'oasis'. I was shown how to select, pick and arrange the blooms in a dozen vases containing crunched-up wire, to make the Residency interior in itself a bower of scents and colour.

Sometimes, according to the weather, I picked them in the evening and kept the flowers fresh in buckets of water on the back verandah. For this I had the help of an old bandy-legged *bhisti* water-carrier who followed me every-where when on the task, emptied the old vases for me, filled them with fresh water and cleared up my messes or I would never had got through the daily task. When I began to get the hang of the language we used to hold long conversations on gardening during these sessions, and it was obvious that though humble and poor he loved his work in the Residency garden and took great pride in the

The author cutting flowers to decorate the Residency

beautiful blooms he produced. He told me he had been born and had lived all his life on one of the skiff *doungas* tied in their hundreds to the back-waterways of the Jhelum River. Many children drowned, he said. 'Are they not taught to swim?' I asked, horrified. 'Water is for washing and drinking. We do not swim,' he said simply, 'only the burra Canon sahib make boys swim.'

The little *mali* would compliment me occasionally on my handiwork when he thought I had done a job particularly well. When on the few occasions that both Sheila and I were indisposed together he could do the flowers perfectly adequately himself, but he would not touch them if we were around. Flower arranging was the memsahibs' job! Most exacting and perhaps the one I enjoyed doing most, was inventing new devices of low spreading arrangements on the long dining table for a dinner party. Sheila would tell me the colour scheme she wanted for that evening. Then she left it to me.

The vase which caused me the most trouble and which took the longest to arrange, was a spectacular Chinese one of ancient beauty bought in Peking which stood at the bottom of the wide, polished and uncarpeted staircase which shallowly ascended between ornately carved balustrades. The stairs, directly up to half landing from the square entrance hall, rose on to the full height of the house. The precious vase stood on a stand by the lower step. I was always afraid it would one day topple over and break into smithereens. Nothing, in those days in India, anyway that I ever came across, was insured. In any case this vase was probably too valuable to insure! Neither was wire netting much good for such a deep narrow-necked vase. I kept the flowers going as long as possible by daily cutting out and replenishing.

Once this vase had been seen to I could relax and enjoy the arrangements for the drawing-room situated to the left of the hall. This beautifully proportioned room had a row of French windows leading to balconies on two sides with the side away from the front overlooking a neat croquet lawn. All the windows were framed in deep pink brocade curtains. The ceiling of the room was painted in an unusual turquoise which picked out the colour of a fine circular carpet in the centre of the floor. The embroidery worked and lined carpet was especially designed for Sheila by the well-known Hadow's firm of Srinagar.

This lovely room was full of Sheila's personal touches, and everywhere, of course, were vases, some nailed to the pale pink walls to trail flowers and greenery. Other small vases stood on tables beside silver framed and signed photographs of magnificently bejewelled Maharajas, and there was one of Sheila in a long white dress and feathers on the occasion of her Court presentation. For these small tables in the pink-drawing room, I liked to arranged giant sweet-peas in mauves and lavenders.

ϔ   ϔ   ϔ   ϔ

30

The drawing-room of the Residency

31

Most of my other duties were also with Sheila. The all-important Book, which reposed in the smaller of the two Lodges, was brought in by late afternoon when the gates were closed, and was quickly glanced through to see if anyone of particular interest had signed during the day. Next morning I went over it in detail and consulted Sheila and Dem before making any moves.

Everyone who signed was asked to something. I typed out the names under the headings of either Luncheon, Buffet Lunch, Tea & Tennis/Croquet, Cocktails or Dinner. Guests were sent invitations strictly according to rank with the exception of personal friends who were siphoned in. The least important in rank were relegated to cocktails which were, to me, more fun than formal luncheon or dinner party. I wrote the invitation cards out by hand and gave them to one or other of the *chaprassis* for delivery.

Next, Sheila and I got down to advance invitations to officials who through the holiday season of spring and early summer expected annually to be invited to stay on their way to fishing or climbing camps. These visits were arranged months in advance through their personal secretaries. Then there were the last minute requests of VIPs which had to be fitted in somehow. The Viceroy and party came every year and sometimes more than once so popular was Kashmir. Governors had a habit of arriving at the busiest time of year on some urgent business after which they invariably set off for the mountains on leave. It was an endless headache for Sheila to fit them all in and not offend those who had to be reallocated to stay in a lesser official's house because some Bishop or such like was coming at short notice. Not the least of her headaches was the tricky protocol of the seating arrangements at the table, and heaven help the hostess if she mistakenly demoted a guest in favour of a more junior one! All this protocol business seemed to me to be laughable, but one case I found appealing. For six months a bride in India had the right to be chief guest. Many were the blushing brides returning from honeymoon in the mountains of Kashmir who enjoyed the honour of sitting on the right hand side of Dem!

Every Monday Sheila came into my office where de Mello would be waiting to be primed well ahead on future dates about the numbers for meals, rooms to be got ready and so on. He took no notes but stored it all in his head. I never knew him to forget or make a blunder. Next in came de Souza carrying book and pencil for the menus for the following week. Sheila, who was an excellent cook herself, after praising his latest masterpiece, would listen to his suggestions, from time to time making a few amendments and variations. The food served was always absolutely first class cuisine, the sweets beautifully decorated.

※　　※　　※　　※

Side view of Residency showing balconies; note croquet lawn

33

On my first night there was a dinner party. It was already chilly when night fell, and after changing into a long dress and coming down into the drawing-room I found the log fire therein lit. The two dogs lay toasting themselves before it so close that they were in danger of singeing their fur. Ronnie ordered them to move back. I hardly recognized her all dressed up with her short wiry hair neatly brushed off her face. She lit up and stood leaning one elbow on the mantelpiece while talking to a Mr Apcar, a wealthy old world widower with courtly manners who had come to live in Srinagar on his retirement from the Punjab.

I was introduced to him and to a Captain Michael Dixon the Political Officer newly arrived, tall and thin in his dinner jacket and black tie and nearly as green as I. With him was his pretty fair wife. I gathered they had only recently been married, and that the Lodge beyond the Cottage was their first home. Both, I noticed, seemed shy and ill at ease, and knowing that one of my tasks was to help 'make the party go', I related my near birth story on the journey up which indeed did bring forth a giggle from Patsy.

Half the trouble for the stickiness of the party that evening was not only the Dixons' shyness and myself a newcomer yet to learn the ropes, but that Sheila was not feeling well. She had told me on coming down the stairs that she had been having giddy attacks which were disconcerting to say the least especially as people might construe it as having too much drink taken, a condition she was not prone to. She was determined to keep going until the Viceregal visit was over when she would consult the Residency Surgeon as to the cause. Looking at her it was hard to believe she was not well. Pink cheeked she looked the picture of health in a buttercup-yellow low cut gown tight about her full figure.

The eighth member for dinner was a drawn - looking, pale under his tan, subaltern with a heavily bandaged arm in a sling. We were served sherries before dinner, and only one glass each at that, and promptly the small company was ushered across the hall to the dining-room, down the middle of which gleamed a candle-lit table capable of being extended to seat many more. Sheila had told me that she was making tapestry seats for the matching walnut chairs and had still some way to go to complete the set. All the furniture in this room was of Kashmir walnut. The tables depicted a bank of small carved Persian flowers and leaves running round the edges, the work of local craftsmen. The long curtains at the windows were in a soft orange colour, and the floor rugs, chainstitched by Hadow's, had been made to match in their beige, orange and greens which colour scheme blended in delightfully with the light wood.

Two Muslim *khitmagars* waited on us under de Mello's alert eyes. Both waiters wore the red and gold wide cummerbund round their waists with similar coloured cross bands in their *pugris*.

Patsy sat in the place of honour beside Dem while I sat on his other side, the subaltern on my left. 'Just my luck to get shot at by a sniper's bullet when there is a real war on at home,' the young man remarked as we sat down.

'On the North West Frontier? How romantic!' I said, thinking, good he can talk about it. I had not liked to ask.

'Romantic my foot, or rather my arm. It's dashed painful I can tell you.'

'Oh, that's rotten. Don't they give you pain killers... or, or something?'

'Not enough, the wretches. Once you're out of hospital you're supposed to just get on with it. I could do with some *bhang* right now.'

'What's that?'

'Dope the men take before going into battle. One sherry's not enough,' he expressed whimsically.

'There's some in the soup,' I said tasting my consommé served in Chinese bowls, 'and wine to come. I daresay you can go great on the Port later. That's what they used to give wounded soldiers in the Mutiny, so I've read. Srinagar must be a nice place to convalesce in.'

'Not a bit. It's damned boring. You're the first unattached female I've met in three weeks. There's nothing doing up here at this time of year unless you can go shooting, and I can't even hold a gun.

'Did you sign your name in the book?'

'Yes. Colonel Fraser used to know my father. Same Regiment. I'm raring to get back to it. Pretty worried they'll be posted to the Middle East without me.'

I watched him coping awkwardly with the porcelain soup spoon. 'I'll cut up the next course for you,' I observed.

I did. It was a whole partridge each, (known in the country as *chikor*) with all the accoutrements of fried breadcrumbs, bread sauce and the thinnest of fried potatoes. He tackled his plate with a fork.

'I did not realize there was a war on in India,' I resumed the conversation, surprised that Dem had not mentioned it at our morning session. 'Tell me more.'

'Local skirmishes rather than out and out war. Going on for so long nobody has bothered to report it since Churchill's young days - that is unless an officer gets killed,' the intriguing young man explained while jabbing unsuccessfully into a potato chip. He chased it round the plate until with a grimace he gave up and took to his fingers, 'just another incident on the North West Frontier sort of attitude. Actually the whole area has blown up again because of that old fanatic the Fakir of Ipi. He deliberately inflames the tribes against the British. We are supposed to be guarding the outposts of the Empire against the Mongol hordes, or some such, to keep the supply lines in Waziristan open. What happens is that the tribesmen gather in their thousands periodically to have a go. The Pathan loves a fight and fights for the sheer heck of it. They are taught to do so from childhood and are spoiling to have a shot at whoever comes along be it us or some innocent merchantman on the trade route plying his wares. When the tribesman gets too much of a nuisance or succeeds in capturing a strategic position on the heights guarding a pass, we mount a full scale operation. The adrenalin fairly flows. Great fun - until one gets hit...' the young man's voice trailed off. I glanced at him. His face looked pinched.

35

'What happened in your case?'

'We had attacked and dislodged them and they were rapidly scattering into the mountains when one turned to give a parting shot - at me personally, I reckon! Pathans are absolutely crack shots, you know, seldom miss.'

'You see, Evelyn,' came in Dem who had been listening-in to the latter part of the tale, 'there's nothing much for the tribesmen to live off in those bare mountains, so the Government pays the Pathan a subsistence allowance and hopes he'll behave. However it is part of their way of life to come down from their fastnesses every now and then to raid the lower villages for food and girl wives. To punish them for the havoc caused to innocent people, the Government cuts off their allowance; this causes them to do a bit more raiding than before, and so it goes on in a vicious circle. Just the same when I was serving in Bannu after the First World War.'

'You must speak Pashtu fluently, sir. I'm struggling with it,' sighed the subaltern.

'Plenty of enlisted Pathans in your Regiment to practise on,' laughed Dem, 'you'll soon get the hang of it.'

'Do you mean to say they enlist to fight their own people?' Patsy asked blue eyes wide.

'Why sure,' chipped in Mr Apcar from across the table, 'inter-tribal vendettas can last for a hundred years up there. Great men, the Pathans, haughty and defiant, proud of their faith in Islam and the teaching of their Mullahs. Prepared to fight for their faith every inch of the way. Great sense of humour too.'

'My bearer is a Pathan,' Sheila revealed. 'We sent him down to Bombay to collect Evelyn.'

'To begin with I was quite scared of him' I opened up, 'but I soon found myself being treated like the baby which I am here.'

'Once you've learnt the language...' Dem began.

'Give her a chance,' interrupted Sheila.

'You either toughen up or this country kills you,' Ronnie had her say. 'I can't see anything tough about this way of living,' Michael put in looking appreciatively at the next course.

It was a sweet fit for royalty of delectable home made ice-cream with fresh fruit set in crunchy meringue, the whole decorated with a candyfloss of shiny burnt sugar woven into a fairy basket of so delicate a pattern it seemed a crime to break into it. The 'angels on horseback' savoury to follow of flaked almonds embedded in a prune which itself was enveloped in crisp bacon upon a golden crunch of fried bread, was also perfection - and this was only an 'informal' dinner. What would it be like when the Viceroy came?

Sheila caught Patsy's eye and we ladies repaired upstairs to powder our noses while the men left alone with their port no doubt regaled one another with their *shikar* exploits either of bird or Pathan. Before joining us in the drawing-room they walked out into the night to 'water' the borders. Apparently this relic of Mess dinners in India came from the times when there were no inside conveniences. Now the men passed the door to the modern 'gents' on their way out. Though I never thought of myself as a prude, it struck me as an extraordinarily crude ending to a most civilized evening! Thus I was amused when Mr Apcar on later taking his leave used the very words that had come into my mind.

'I live on a houseboat across the way from here,' he said bowing low over my hand, 'and I very much hope that the Resident and his lady will honour me by bringing the charming Miss-sahibs over the water to dinner so that I can show you how civilized such a crude home can be!'

Huh! I smiled to myself. The wide flowing Jhelum River, with its seven famous bridges built on wooden piles through the picturesque town, was a well known drain for the inhabitants. Did the civilized gentlemen who lived on their houseboats add to the pollution by 'watering' it after their dinners?

5
Viceroys and the Shikar

The tension was terrific. Nerves were strung up every bit as much as if they had been royalty itself - indeed they *were* royalty in India.

We were given instructions as to how to behave. The men in the household were not to bend from the waist but to bow the head from the neck; we Miss-sahibs were shown by a knowledgeable Sheila how to make a curtsey with one foot placed before the other. It was not all that easy to achieve smoothly. We practised away until Sheila passed the performances.

At last the great day dawned. We found ourselves lined up on the steps of the Residency for the visit of Their Excellencies the Viceroy and the Marchioness of Linlithgow, their daughter and entourage. After what seemed like hours of waiting, the exalted guests swept up the drive in a fleet of cars which had come over the Banihal Pass in the mighty Pir Panjal Range. They disgorged, each one seemingly taller than the last. I was so astounded at their combined great heights which gave the appearance of a phalanx of Goliaths, that when my turn came to be introduced I completely forgot all about curtseying and gave each a hearty handshake instead. Ever selfconscious of my own above average tallness for a girl in those days, I was delighted to find myself topped by so many. Even Lady Jane Hope, the smallest of the group, was a six footer.

'You didn't curtsey,' stated Ronnie out of the side of her mouth after she had risen from hers.

'You don't have to remind me,' I hissed back, chagrined that I had let the side down, a blush of shame spreading over my face. Fortunately Dem and Sheila were so preoccupied in ushering their guests into the house that my omission failed to register, but one of the ADCs appeared to give me an icy aristocratic nose-in-air stare as he passed by.

A naval officer's daughter myself, I had never thought very highly of the Army with their drab khaki uniforms and comic Charlie Chaplin moustaches. Give me a clean-shaven naval officer in speckless attire with shining gold braid every time. *They* were my romantic beau ideal! Yet I had always believed equerries must be a particularly fine brand of men. On this occasion the ADCs certainly looked the part. Each matched the Linlithgows in height (perhaps they had been especially chosen for 'the girls'), all with broad shoulders well braced-back. Super men indeed, and here I had already failed the test as the frosty blue eyes in a handsome acquiline face had clearly indicated.

However there was little time to dwell on my short-comings as their Excellencies were escorted up the staircase and led along the landing to the imposing Viceregal suite overlooking the garden. The twin beds therein had only just been delivered in time. On instructions from Delhi new ones had been made specifically extra-long for the visit. There the beds lay serenely pristine under their brand new brocade covers ready to receive the giants.

The real *raison d'être* of the autumn visit was, of course, for the *shikar*. The famed Hokra Jheel, owned by the Maharaja of Kashmir, was considered to be the best duck shoot in the sub-continent, and it was situated in one of the most spectacular spots in the world. For this prized occasion those from the Residency were the guests of HH, the guns all hand picked. The party retired to bed at a reasonable hour the evening before the first shoot so that all would be rested and in good fettle to start out early the next morning.

It was the first time I had set eyes on Hari Singh, to whom I had already typed some letters. In the early light I looked curiously at this man who had been so badly used in his youth by an Englishman to make him for the rest of his life conscious that many were sniggering behind his back for being the thinly disguised Mr 'A' of the worldwide reported trial. Poor Prince, I thought, taking in His Highness, now a large tall man, his high-buttoned three-quarter length *achkan* tight over stomach, his figure topped by a small pork pie hat to give him a pear-shaped look. He wore dark glasses, comparatively unusual in those days. Did he wear them to hide his dislike of being stared at? Perhaps he wore them to cover his undoubted shyness. Whatever the cause there was nothing wrong with his eyesight: he was a magnificent shot, none better in the land. The VIPs, united in their enthusiasm, expertise and keeness for the sport, had gathered other like-minded men around them, and the result was fantastic - and to me, my first shoot on such a scale, barbaric.

As spectators Ronnie and I sat on the lake shore with the ladies (Sheila was with the men - the only female gun) watching the other members of the shooting party being paddled out to hides about a quarter of a mile apart along the edges of the great *jheel*. Each individual had two guns, a loader and a thousand cartridges.

In the early morning light the scene was one not easily forgotten as the autumn mists slowly lifted to reveal hills and valleys flushed with a rosy glow reflected in glimpses of calm patches of pond. All around us where we sat were reeds and high bulrushes, and up and above and way over as far as the eye could see were the encircling mountains, range upon range of them. The mists on the main waters were the last to lift. Almost suddenly the vapours vanished, gone, and there before us we saw a huge expanse of water crowded with quietly resting duck who had flighted in from Siberia. Habitually they stayed days or weeks before moving on southwards. Their places were taken in a stream by more flights from the north. They swooped in, in high formation and gracefully landed with a fluffing and flashing of feathered wings, the air laden with their joyful quacks, geese giving their distinctive 'honk'.

His Highness, the Maharaja of Kashmir's arrival on King's Birthday Party

40

Now, as quietly the guns rested in their places, there was utter silence, a time of tranquillity in the lifting dawn when no-one spoke. Then one single shot rang out. Within seconds all hell was let loose. With a battering of wings the sky became thick with every kind of wild fowl as they took to the air in alarm: geese, widgeon, teal, grey-lags, pintails, mallard... in their thousands they rose with a thrashing of wings to darken the early morning sky into darkness again. The crouching guns waited for the birds to swing over their way. Then the sound of wings was obliterated by a tremendous fusillade. It seemed to me watching, as I in defence put my hands up to my ears, that here you did not have to be a good shot; that in this sky black with birds one could scarcely miss.

Every now and then there was a lull; then another and another flight came over. There was an hour's pause for a picnic lunch which was more like a banquet where we, HH's guests, were served right royally in a *shamiana* marquee by the fleet of servants.

Before the afternoon's shooting started up, Ronnie and I, on the excuse of getting back to our duties, took our leave and slipped away in one of the chauffeur driven cars. It was quiet in the Residency garden when we returned, blissfully quiet and peaceful in our shaded garden where in the stillness we could listen to the chirping and trills of bird song.

I had not been prepared for a shoot of such magnitude, indeed I had scarcely been on a shoot at all. I felt what I had just witnessed was a massacre out there on the Hokra *jheel* by the invitation of Sir Hari Singh. And massacre it was to me when I saw the mound of feathered birds laid out on the lawn each so prettily and variedly marked, their broken necks dangling pathetically.

Though I had never particularly liked the idea of shooting and was glad the opportunity to learn had never come my way, I had not before felt sickened as I did now. Though Ronnie saw how I felt, her love of animals and particularly of dogs, who were children with souls to her and heaven would not be heaven without allowing them in, did not extend to the same extent to feathered beasts as long as they were cleanly shot. I did not voice my feelings then to the Frasers - though I did later on the subject of larger game particularly the delicate startled deer and the powerful rippling-muscled tiger in the jungles. If others felt like me in India in 1939 they mostly kept quiet about it. I felt myself to be a total nit-wit and knew such an extraordinary un-British view would be regarded with unbelief if not scorn. As a newcomer I believed myself to be unnaturally squeamish.

However, secretly 'anti' from the time of that great Hokra shoot, I was not such an aesthete that I was not all for the culinary results. The birds were put in the 'freezer'. This was a round house which stood at the back of the Residency. It was dug down to below ground level and lined with alternative blocks of ice and straw. With the ban on beef and everyone satiated with mutton and the small tough chickens, any form of game was relished. Kept in its round larder, the birds remained frozen right into the following summer, by which time they had been mostly used up.

But to go back to the evening of that first outing, the shooting party returned tired and exhilarated to find fires lit. The men stood with their backs before the drawing-room fire sipping their whiskeys and telling their stories of the day, satisfied that it had been a good one - one of the best. The Resident and the Viceroy alone had each come near to the single record bag of a thousand birds each, a sum which HH was believed to have surpassed though no one knew exactly as his and his henchman's bags had been removed to the Lake Palace.

'The record for the season up here stands at 10,000 for one gun,' I heard Dem inform an ADC whose first visit it was.

'How many did your wife bag, sir?' another asked.

'A hundred,' Dem answered proudly.

'Really? A hundred! Jolly good show. Must be a record for a female gun.'

All this excited talk of records left me unimpressed. I found more enjoyable the expeditions out to the rice paddy fields to watch driven snipe jinking and zig-zagging across the rice. They were so small they looked like sparrows. To bring one of these fast little birds down needed great skill, and even with all the experts in the field during the Viceroy's visit, those bags were small.

On other days, and further afield, I climbed up the hills with the men to watch them shoot *chikor*, the red-legged, greyish-brown hill partridge, not unlike a large French partridge. As quietly we waited we listened to their deep-toned call from way up in the mountains. Then the beaters could be heard coming nearer with cries of 'mark Sahib' as the large birds rocketed like cannon down towards the guns. They came so fast that many drummed over to the safety of the lower mustard fields, where they squatted, invisible. These birds too made most delicious eating, as did quail. But snipe was always the favourite savoury. Served on crisp toast, their long beaks were turned like a spit to skewer their little bodies. Use of fingers was permissible. The whole bird was eaten, even the head, the tiny brain being considered a particular delicacy. Only the beaks were left on scraped plates when fingers were dipped in scented lacquer finger bowls.

ᛟ   ᛟ   ᛟ   ᛟ

The Viceregal visit was going extremely well. Indeed it could be said to be a huge success with smiles all round, and even the ADCs turned out to be human after all cracking jokes and relating tall tales to much laughter. Her Excellency was charming to us staff, relaxed and appreciative, and His Excellency was in great humour; the shooting he so enjoyed he declared to be 'superb'. Everything, in fact, was going like clockwork much to the relief of Sheila who was putting on a brave face to hide her tiredness. Then, towards the end of the visit, something perfectly frightful occurred.

A 'chikor drive' with HH

It happened at dinner in the long dining-room. The glowing walnut table was extended to its fullest; the candles threw flickering light onto the lacey carving admired round the table's edges. The seating was arranged so that Dem and Sheila sat opposite one another in the middle with their Excellencies at their respective sides. The rest of the house party and guests sat in diminishing importance of PAs and APAs and their wives to ADCs and such lowly members as Miss-sahibs at the ends of the table. Suddenly there was an upset. De Mello, the up to then perfect, suave, and unflappable butler, in a fit of exhausted nerves, inadvertently tilted the dish of peas he was holding over Lady Linlithgow's shoulder into the satin lap of her dress. There was a sudden hush around the table.

'My God,' breathed the aghast ADC on my left, 'that'll put the kibosh on this trip.'

'Her Ex will never forget that!' groaned the nice young man on my other side. '*That* is unforgiveable!' Open-mouthed I watched the sight of Her Excellency with a most definitely NOT amused wave of hand glittering with rings brushing the offending vegetables off the expensive folds of her dress. They scattered all round her, most onto the floor, others over the table. The stunned silence round the company was broken by an agonized gasp from the distracted de Mello. This was quickly followed by a flurry of *khitmagars* and minions from the kitchen rushing to fetch pans and brushes to sweep up the bouncing little green balls from off the table and under the illustrious guest's feet.

I thought it was the funniest thing I had ever seen in all my life, and dissolved into giggles. 'She can't be seriously annoyed,' I tittered, 'she *must* be flesh and blood underneath. Oh poor, poor de Mello...'

'My dear girl,' expressed the ADC at my side with raised eyebrow, 'be careful. In these circles that remark could be interpreted as lese-majesty!'

It *was* 'poor de Mello'. He got a fierce ticking off from Dem. As for Sheila, all her well laid successful plans were forgotten. For the rest of the visit she could think of nothing else but the shame of the accident.

6
More VIPs

The next to stay (to luxuriate in the extra size beds!) were the Cassells. He was the Commander-in-Chief, India, known as a 'real soldier's soldier'. To me he was 'Sir Robert' and I could well see how the troops loved him. This visit, to the relief of all and to Sheila and de Mello in particular, went off without a hitch.

But the visit of the Nawab and Begum of Paripur, despite their chatty Indian ADC, an extremely able and delightful man, was, to begin with, decidedly hard work. Even with our combined efforts the conversation with the Nawab and his Begum remained stiff and formal. At meals particularly it was difficult to keep up a flow of talk. The Begum, sweet and lovely, seemed tied up with shyness and hardly uttered a word; indeed at first I did not think she had any English. Her husband always rattled off to her in Hindi, which tongue I found hard to understand. The Begum had only just come out of purdah. It explained her reticence where men were concerned, and why when Dem addressed her she froze. I longed to ask her about her life in the Zenana but felt it would have been an impertinence to try and delve further, and I kept to the safe subject of her children.

However the thaw came in tennis with the Nawab and his ADC who both played an excellent game. Sheila was not fit enough to play. Ronnie did not play; so I partnered Dem versus the Indians. Dem had a natural eye for a ball. He played tennis up to County standard and was an International at polo with a handicap of eight. He was in HH's polo team as well as playing cricket with him; both pastimes were great plusses in his relationship with the Maharaja.

Though I say it, I was not too bad at the game myself having been coached throughout childhood in France. Dressed in a white divided skirt of those days worn with aertex shirt, and the men perfectly turned out in white flannel trousers and crisp shirts with the sleeves rolled up, the 'Oh good shot' 'Well served' and 'Bad luck' were fairly bandied about. Two small boys known as '*goliwallahs*' retrieved the balls for us. Gamely and efficiently they ran bare-footed in calf length puttees around the asphalt court. They looked exact miniature replicas of the older servants with their little red and gold slashed *pugris*.

In between these hard hitting games we joined Sheila and the Begum under the chenar trees to cool down with refreshing drinks of *nimbu pani* which de Souza made with squeezed limes boiled with water and sugar, allowed to cool, and then served very cold with a dash of mint. On these occasions when all was relaxed I found that the Begum could speak perfectly adequate English.

Sheila with HH at Residency on King's Birthday Party.

❦　　❦　　❦　　❦

One autumn visitor of great interest was the fascinating teller of outback tales Sir Mark Aurel Stein, the famed Anglo-Hungarian archaeologist, explorer of Chinese Turkestan, and Principal of the Oriental College in Lahore, a still vigorous man then in his old age. Knowing his passion for the hills and mountains, Dem arranged a day expedition to spy out the 'Ursa Thibetanus' known locally as *Kala Bhalu*, the Himalayan black bear feared for his ferocity.

On the chosen day, we were driven out towards the Sannowat mountains where at road-head we left the cars. A *shikari* tracker led us in single file quite a climb up the steep hillside to some open land just above tree level. In spring the bears came down to feed on the long grass in these sheep folds. In summer they came further down still to eat the maize and corn in the lower fields and to chew the ripe apricots and walnuts from off the farmer's trees. Steadily we climbed on and up. We then hid behind great patches of rhododendrons.

'In summer these valleys are alive with bears eating the ripe mulberries,' Dem informed low voiced as we squatted down. 'The *Kala Bhalu* is rather smaller than the Red Bear though far more dangerous when suddenly surprised.'

'I saw some terrible injuries inflicted on a farmer and his wife last summer,' Ronnie vouchsafed. 'The man was badly mauled and the woman had her face almost scalped off.'

'You tell me that now,' I said with a shiver.

'Dem is armed with a rifle,' soothed Sir Mark as he scanned the hillside with his binoculars. 'You know I once saw a black bear climbing a tree. He got wind of me and almost fell out in a near ball he was in such a hurry to get away! My goodness he moved fast downhill travelling at an enormous rate for such a lumbering looking beast. Quite amazing.'

'They can weigh five hundred pounds and more,' Dem took up, 'Enormous muscular development, and they can take an extraordinary amount of lead if not in a vital spot.'

'You're not going to shoot today?' I frowned.

'Not unless we are attacked,' grinned Dem seeing my unease. 'Don't worry, their powers of hearing are only fair. Their eyesight and sense of smell make up for this though, unlike the black sloth bear found in the plains which has very poor eyesight.' We all thoughtfully relapsed into silence.

After quite a period when I was beginning to think we would not see a bear that day and began to wonder if they existed up there, the *shikari* pointed to our left with a murmured, '*kala bhalu, sahib.*'

All binoculars shifted. Through mine I spotted a male of heavy build with a white horse-shoe marking on his chest. He was a magnificent beast, deep glossy black in colour, about six foot in height, small tail, with fur short and close. I could feel the hair at the back of my neck standing up in excitement, awe and admiration. He was on his own. For a long while we watched his every movement as he fed. Then he ambled on further away. Scanning the far ridges we watched some *ghoral*, short curving-horned wild mountain goat, quite rare to see even in those parts indigenous to them. We then relaxed and unpacked our picnic tea while still seated in the shelter of the rhododendron bushes.

'Across those mountains you can pick out the trails made by the Gujars where the tribal nomads come down in their caravans from their high pasture-land,' reminisced Sir Mark. 'Their tents and cooking pots are carried by ponies with swinging bells round their necks, an unforgettable sound which you hear long before you can see them. The sound continues after they have passed, fading, fading... Ah, to be young again and to travel with them!'

'What happens when *they* get old?' I asked.

'When they cannot follow any longer they are left to die by the wayside. Seems cruel, but when you think of it not a bad way to go alone with the mountain sounds around. A mercifully quick death too in the freezing cold. Would suit me...'

We all fell silent once again and pensive in the glorious wilds of those bear haunted hills. At last with the sun sinking we tore ourselves away to descend to the lower slopes where the silver birches glowed red in the slanting rays of the sunset, and the valley was full of russet-browns from the wild cherry and apricot trees. Everywhere one looked old man's beard could be seen draped softly like fine grey cashmere shawls over bushes red with rose hips.

᭄   ᭄   ᭄   ᭄

There were many other guests who came to stay when the spring and early summer season of holidaying up from the plains was in full swing the next year. Then lakes were crowded with houseboats full of families and young people. I particularly remember the Bishop of Lahore and Mrs Barnes, and also 'Doc' Holland as he was affectionately known who became Sir Henry. He was the Missionary eye surgeon with the squeaky voice said to have so become through singing on as a choir boy when his voice was breaking. He was famed throughout India as the miracle doctor who in Baluchistan and other north-western parts restored the sight of thousands with his cataract operations. But the VIP visit that Ronnie and I enjoyed the most, was that of the Governor of Bombay with Lady Lumley and their stunning aide Major Richardson. We decided that we liked the latter best of all because, as a mature man, he did not look down his nose at PAs!

Governors in India were nearly as important as Viceroys, the only difference being that one did not bow or curtsey to them. Therefore much care was taken in preparing for this visit. Sheila, for days before, was on tenterhooks lest the 'pea episode', as it had become known, should repeat itself, or worse! In fact the visit went off as if on oiled wheels. But it had a sequel.

48

They came towards the end of the hectic season and just before the weather hotted up to its 90° plus Fahrenheit of high summer. At the May-June sublime time of year the most popular form of entertainment at the Residency became fork luncheons for up to a hundred or so guests in the colourful garden setting. Carpets were spread out on the lawns, and small tables with chairs were dotted around. To one side, under the chenars, lay a length of white damask covered trestle tables on which a sumptuous buffet concocted by de Souza was laid.

To help him prepare the food on these bumper occasions, de Souza had his *matis* or minions, usually from the bazaar and very often the servants' relations of whom all told they made quite a village, living in the *godowns* at the back. They were not paid but were given 'perks' in kind by de Souza and de Mello from the Resident's bountiful table. The system worked very well. They were the responsibility of the particular retainer, and whenever further help was needed whether out of doors or in the house there was never any lack of volunteers to hand.

The food of course was superb. More often than not the menu was of quails in aspic to begin with and 'Fasinjan' to follow. This was an Afghan dish of chicken cooked in pomegranate juice with crushed walnuts added. As an alternative was the maestro's own special rich cold curry dish with the rice, starkly simple and cooked to exact perfection, served separately. Chocolate gâteau and fresh fruit salad with whipped chantilly cream followed to complete the gourmet meal. If de Souza was the maestro, it was Sheila who was the inspirer with her book of recipes collected over the years, some inherited from her mother's and her mother-in-law's times in India as far back as the last century.

Naturally everyone tucked in with a will while unobtrusively Sheila sailed round the garden in one of her pretty dresses and introduced the guests to one another. As they rose to replenish their plates the company was asked to change their places to new tables for the next course. Into this delightfully informal scene the Lumleys arrived to mix with all and give the occasion that extra *bon-ton* that came with Governors. For one thing, to say one had actually lunched with one such high-up and his lady was quite something to be able to off-handedly drop into a future conversation!

On this occasion the Lumleys' visit was for two nights only. The prime reason for their coming to Srinagar was for leave at a fishing camp up in the mountains beyond the village of Achibal. After they left there was a lull in the entertainment, and Dem and Sheila seized the opportunity to take leave themselves and go into camp for a break. Ronnie and I were left behind to hold the fort.

During the season the sheer number of people signing in the Book made it difficult to invite the young to more than a cocktail party during which hubbub there was little opportunity to get to know anyone individually. I had grumbled to Ronnie that I never met anyone who was not less than twice my age. I was now able to rectify this by inviting one or two unmarried girls to the Residency, which led to joining a crowd of young men for bathing picnics on the house-boats on the lakes. I enjoyed myself hugely and in no time had one or two tentative proposals of marriage which were turned down. Nothing could come up to being PA at the Kashmir Residency!

As could happen so quickly in the Vale, one tennis party was broken up by a sudden storm of gale force winds followed by pelting rains during which the leaves were torn in strips from the chenar trees to lie strewn thickly over the lawns. The rain continued to pour down all that night and all the next day. On the second night of incessant rain while Ronnie and I were on our own at dinner at the round table in the bay window waited on by my ever favourite Dost Mohammed, a message came from Major Richardson to say that Lady Lumley had been taken ill. A doctor and nurse were urgently needed. They could not move her from camp as the violent thunderstorms in the mountains had carried away a succession of bridges, and landslides had obliterated parts of the track. They were totally cut off from transport. The situation was dire. Would the Resident send out a rescue party as quickly as possible?

Ronnie and I looked at one another. The Resident was not there! Neither was Major Hailey, the next senior man under Dem, nor Michael Dixon, and the Political Agent was up in Gilgit. Rising to the crisis, Ronnie and I leapt into action. We got on to Captain Ledgard, the Residency Surgeon, who together with the English matron of the small Srinagar Nursing Home, a Mrs Hempster, promptly set forth in two cars with drugs, mackintoshes, umbrellas and boots. It was some days before we heard what happened next:

By the time Captain Ledgard's party got to Achibal, the *katcha* (rough) unmade-up road from thereon into the mountains had become a river bed. The first car got stuck in the mud. Revving, pushing, shoving, laying down fir branches, digging, only made matters worse as the wheels skidded and the vehicle sank deeper and deeper into the mire. Abandoning that one they put chains on the other, transferred everything from the first car, and, overloaded, started off again in the torrential rain. After two-and-a-half hours of skidding and sliding and pushing, they had made so little progress that they called a halt to take stock. It was obvious that the situation they were in was hopeless. The doctor decided to walk back in the sleeting rain to ring for more help. This he did past the abandoned car and on to the nearest phone in Achibal. Luckily the line was still functioning, and he got through to ask for a rescue party to come out to rescue *them*! He then proceeded to retrace his steps.

Not far up the track, Captain Ledgard found the wooden bridge he had just crossed over had been swept away by the foaming torrent that the river had become. Impossible as it was at that spot to wade over, he clambered up along the bank until he found a shallower place. Taking his life in his hands he waded

50

over. By now soaking wet through and through, he sat down on the far bank to empty his boots of water before carrying on. The downpour, if anything, was worse than ever. When at last he struggled up to the further car expecting to find Mrs Hempster and the driver waiting in it, he found their Excellencies and Major Richardson also seated therein looking like drowned rats. Taking the doctor aside the anxious Matron informed him that Lady Lumley had a very high temperature and was in a delirium.

Apparently when help had failed to reach them, and fearful that his wife might not survive another night in camp, Sir Roger and Major Richardson made the decision to move her. The servants and the men in the fishing camp had slipped, slithered and stumbled down the boggy track for miles carrying Lady Lumley in an improvised litter.

The five Europeans now had to endure a most uncomfortable night in the car, the men filthy with mud and soaked to the skin while the tempest continued to rage around them. Lightning crashed down in forked javelins, thunder roared overhead, and the river alongside became a raging rising torrent which threatened to carry them and their car away at any moment. The *shikaris* and servants from the camp sat huddled on their hunkers under the trees, the whites of their terrified eyes lit up in the brilliant flashes.

Sir Roger Lumley said afterwards that he had never been so frightened in all his life as he was that night of storm and tempest, lightning and crashing trees. His fears for their safety were added to by his wife's incoherent speech and ravings as he tried to hold her quiet. No one slept a wink. The only good thing that could be said about that nightmare time was that the drugs Captain Ledgard administered to the patient began to take effect and her temperature was at least no longer round the thermometer top.

Early next morning the rescue party which had gathered in Achibal, sent *tongas* up to the broken bridge. From there they led ponies across the river to the stranded cars. Lady Lumley was lifted out and held on one of the ponies led by coolies. She was negotiated over the bridgeless torrent with her husband, the doctor, matron and Major Richardson close behind. They all crossed to the far bank safely. Once there Lady Lumley was bundled into a tonga for Achibal from where the bedraggled group were speedily driven off in waiting cars. Lady Lumley was taken straight to the Nursing Home in Srinagar, where she was diagnosed as having a severe attack of dysentery for which treatment was immediately begun.

Ronnie and I knew none of this as we anxiously waited at the Residency for news. In answer to ours we had received no messages from Dem in his camp even higher up than the Lumleys though further to the west. The first thing we knew of the outcome was the appearance of a very bedraggled Governor and his Aide on the Residency steps in late afternoon. We ordered hot baths to be run for them, told them to come down to supper warm in the Resident's pyjamas and dressing-gown, plus a *choga* (Tibetan or Gilgit cloak) belonging to me and bought from a Chinaman from over the trade route tops. We plied them with double whiskeys and lemons, and sandwiches. I sat on the rug at their feet before the blazing log fire fondling the dogs' ears and listening rapt to the story of their adventure. Late that night, long after the servants had retired, we supported the two men up the stairs to their beds warmed by hot water bottles, and pretty well tucked them in. In no uncertain measure I ordered the Governor of Bombay to stay in bed next day for breakfast. He meekly obeyed.

Though I cannot for the life of me remember the heart-throb Major Richardson's first name - which we no doubt used - the Governor of Bombay became 'Roger' to us, a thing that would never have happened had it not been for the intimacies of the evening to break down all barriers of age and position. Dem and Sheila had the shock of their lives when they returned refreshed from their camp (no message of the drama had got through to them and the weather up there had been merely 'rather bad') to find their exalted guest was on Christian name terms with his personal assistant and the kennel woman!

'Roger' was enjoying himself, but once more he found he was bound by protocol, and protocol in India always won in the end. For such a lengthy stay in his State the Maharaja would have been deeply offended had the Governor not spent part of the time at the Royal Guest House. There, on the lake side, in no doubt luxurious though stiff and starched surroundings, HE Sir Roger Lumley, the Governor of Bombay, and Major Richardson languished, waiting for Lady Lumley to recover which happily she did remarkably quickly considering how seriously ill she had been. Mercifully the rough, wet journey had not further harmed her. And all in good time the intrepid party returned to their camp to resume their interrupted fishing holiday.

7
Ayah, a Munshi and shopping

Ronnie and I shared Ayah. Everyone in India had their own personal servant whether it was a tribesman from the North West Frontier - as was Sheila's Dost Mohammed or an *ayah* from Nepal as was ours, the mother of a clutch of children in the compound. She was the wife of a retired Gurkha *havildar* employed in the household, a man of so upright a bearing it looked as if he wore a brace.

When Ayah was not making our beds, tidying and dusting our rooms, or washing our 'smalls', this plump little woman sat outside our doors in the corridor rapidly knitting. She jumped to her feet whenever we appeared, her face breaking into a dimpled smile to reveal toothless gaps. Shoving her knitting aside she gave us the *namaste* Hindu greeting, palms held together and raised to her forehead with a half bow. She spoke only a few words of Urdu and no English, but we got on famously in sign language. Her bright black eyes watched me closely as I indicated my wishes, her head held slightly to one side. Her stance, unlike her husband's, was backward-leaning on the heels of her sturdy naked feet as if she were large with child, which more often than not she was.

Together we had unpacked on my arrival at the Residency. My room was large with two beds in it. Fitted cupboards ran down the length of one wall so that for the first time since leaving England six months before I was able to fully unpack my cabin trunk, my tin-lined wooden box (it had been in the Hold on board ship) and the four-square second-hand Victorian hat box which had caused such consternation wherever I travelled. Now I could stow my numerous hats and both my summer and winter clothes in the ample space the cupboards provided, after which Ayah called a *chaprassi* to carry the empty trunks away to be put in some out-house. She then stood by, merry eyes resting on my face for what I should want her to do next. When I could not think of anything she did what *she* deemed necessary, even to squeezing a quarter-of-an-inch of toothpaste ready for use on my toothbrush!

Ayah wore a white sari of handspun cotton which invariably slipped down to rest on her shoulders. She would bring it back to her head in an oft repeated graceful move. A nose stud glinted in one nostril, and many bangles of thin silver - used by her babies to cut their teeth on - tinkled on her brown arms. In the evenings before dinner she sprinkled my bath water liberally with scented sandalwood essence of heady perfume, a necessity I gathered to keep my skin from cracking in the high dry atmosphere. The plumbing in The Residency had been modernized though this was still an unusual luxury in any but top people's houses. Ayah herself smelt of the coconut oil which she rubbed into her scalp and long black hair to give it a sleek blue look and keep the grey at bay which it assuredly did. I never saw her with her hair down. By day she wore it tidily tucked up. She was an absolute delight, always beaming, always there, taking everything in with her bright black eyes, and seemingly to enjoy her work. I suppose being an *ayah* (virtually a ladies-maid when such persons were almost extinct) brought great interest into her previous life of following the drum, particularly with two Miss-sahibs who were so very different in character and age. I could see she was sorry for Ronnie who had not married, and as for me she had every hope that I would hurry up and do so before I was too old to have all those *bacchas*!

'*Ghussel taiyar hai?*' I would ask as I rushed in with barely enough time to change for dinner.

'*Taiyar*, Miss-sahib,' she would waddle in from the taps to pick up the clothes I had stepped out of and left on the floor, a thing which was totally against my upbringing but of which Ayah approved. She had got quite cross when at first I attempted to pick them up.

'*Malish*, Miss-sahib?' she enquired as she held the warm towel out after having scrubbed my back in the bath as if I were a child.

'Oh Ayah, there's no time!' But whenever possible I made time before dinner for this delightful relaxation and toning up exercise. For it I would lie face down on the bed while she proceeded to massage shoulders and back, probing out aching muscles, and rubbing my feet with her strong supple hands, her touch banishing tiredness. She could have made a fortune as a masseuse in the West.

'Where did you learn this, Ayah?' I asked into the pillow.

'Ayah not learn,' she giggled, 'Ayah always know. We do all time.'

'Ayah, who taught you to knit?' I asked her on another occasion.

'Ayah not *taught*. Ayah know!' came the answer.

She knitted by the light of nature inborn in her and copied from mother and grandmother for generations right from when she could first hold the needles in her baby hands. She knitted at an incredible speed, patterns being an unknown mystery and anyway unnecessary to her. She would study a picture of a jumper, cardigan, or even a Shetland jersey in a magazine, and in a week or so's time there would be the finished article in the correct size laid out before me exactly as in the design. She never counted stitches; she never even *looked* at them. She used very long needles one of which she held under her armpit. All of us in the Residency wore Ayah's jumpers, her husband and children, of course, and some of the servants too. And there were plenty of people outside who, seeing the results, would ask if we would 'lend' Ayah to them for a jumper. I had come out to India with four dozen silk pairs of stockings in various shades - bought at Harvey Nichols - as I had been forewarned that they were impossible to purchase in Kashmir. When these laddered, as they were always doing, Ayah mended them by knitting them up invisibly with a tiny crochet-hook.

In summer Ayah sat knitting in the shade of the long wooden balcony which connected all the bedrooms at the rear through their French windows. This layout caused much ribald speculation: guests could visit one another at will along it! At any rate there Ayah sat knitting away while chatting incessantly to the *darzi* (tailor) plying his machine by day though he could have scarcely understood her Gurkhali with the odd word of Urdu thrown in. In the evenings before going off duty after turning down my bed and putting my day clothes away and collecting the 'smalls' to wash, she would chat to the *chowkidar* who by that time had arrived. It used to be said that if anyone did, the night-watchman knew what was going on in the Residency bedrooms at night. But we who lived there knew that a good part of the time he was oblivious of anything, for caretaker though he may have been our sleep was punctuated by his snores.

Once when I was invited to a fancy dress Ball at Nedou's Hotel, Ayah spent ten days sitting on the verandah wielding enormous needles to knit 'armour' in tough string so that I could go as Joan of Arc. Sheila had drawn her a sketch of the costume we had in mind, and with one glance at it she was away merrily entering into the spirit of the enterprise. The end result consisted of a long sleeved garment well padded with old stockings on the inside of the shoulders. The legs were knitted up into tights worn over flat pointed shoes. The 'armour' looked most effective when dyed silver - no sprays in those days. The *darzi* made up a tunic to wear over in royal blue velvet with a fleur-de-lys emblem in front painted on by Sheila. Ayah saw me off in this outfit and was as pleased as Punch when I brought back a prize, though surely her fingers must have been made sore by the rough bulky string. I often wondered if she knitted at night in her room in the compound. She must have, to accomplish as much as she did. Besides, the garments brought an aroma of wood smoke and Indian cooking with them until washed out.

The Gurkha couple had a succession of children looked after by a grandmother and 'aunties' who all seemed to live in the compound. I do not remember Ayah or any of the staff having a day off, but they did all get annual leave of two months or so to go to their far flung homes in Nepal, Goa and Chittagong, or the nearby North West Frontier Province where Dost Mohammed had a large family of wives and children. Sheila told me his wives and older children kept the 'farm' going in his absence together with a paid coolie, though farming was hazardous in that barren country which made it imperative for him to earn money, otherwise he would have taken, like so many of his kin, to raiding the more fertile lower villages, and end up a marked man by the British. Instead he worked for them. In a way it suited him. He was enormously respected by the other servants. From my balcony I could hear him at night holding forth about ancient tribal feuds in the fastnesses of his land.

Most of the servants were family men who suffered these long separations during which time they sent back money. Every now and then there was a crisis, and a servant would ask to see Dem in his study with a story of a child dying or some other tragedy for which he urgently needed to go home to the burial. Most reasons were authentic. Some were suspect, too well versed to be genuine as were the favourite excuse of 'my grandfather has fallen down the village well,' or more often still 'my house has burnt down and my children are homeless!' Dem usually let them go. An unhappy or worried servant was no use.

⚜ ⚜ ⚜ ⚜

In the mornings I was awakened by Ayah, a freshly plucked flower in her hair. She brought me a tray of *chota hazri* literally 'little breakfast' of tea and a biscuit or sometimes thin bread and butter and fruit. She would throw wide open the shutters of the French windows to let the sun stream into my room. I was soon up to step out onto the balcony in my newly acquired chiffon dressing gown (Butterfly!) to sniff the scented air from the white jasmine creeping over the lintel, and listen to the sounds from the nearby bazaar, the pi-dogs' barks on the Bund, birds stirring in the trees, the lapping of water onto the *ghat* steps, the call to prayer from the Mosque, voices raised to one another from house-boat to house-boat.

When dressed I descended by the outside wooden steps to the lower balcony where the little *mali* was waiting for me. And together we got down to the first business of the day - the flower arranging.

Then in those early days when everything was new, strange and fascinating, came my time with the *munshi*, lessons which I shared with Patsy for which he charged us the sum of one rupee each a time. (Thirteen rupees to the pound). We sat in a secluded spot in the garden so as not to be distracted by the *chaprassis* on the steps with the continual arrivals and departures. I sucked my pencil expectantly, notebook to hand and feeling like a schoolgirl all over again as I stumbled over the unfamiliar words.

Our *munshi*, who was always just 'Munshi' - we never knew his name in the same way we never knew Ayah's - was a wizened old man who carried an umbrella whatever the weather which showed he was an educated man of means. He wore a *dhoti* of fine white muslin many yards long drawn between his skinny brown legs, and tucked bulkily into his waist. Over this he wore a buttoned-up grey coat, and on his head above steel rimmed spectacles, which seemed not to magnify but to be like planes of glass, perched a pillbox hat. Suspenders held up brightly coloured socks which were immersed into black laced shoes in which his feet swam. He appeared drowned by his clothes, and yet out of the bundle came very correct English exactly enunciated and far more grammatical than our use of our own language. Patsy and I quickly came to appreciate he was an exact teacher who pulled us up for saying 'shall' when it should have been 'will', not to mention our incorrect use of gerunds. Patiently he made us repeat the Urdu

56

words again and again, all the time urging us to pay attention and make a greater effort.

I don't know about Patsy, but I will say that with the phrases being drummed into me day by day, and being able to practise with Ayah and the *mali*, I soon learnt the rudiments, despite behaving in a rather infantile way.

'Memsahib, Miss-sahib, attention please! Repeat after me three times a day *Teen dafa roz roz*. Repeat again: *teen dafa...*'

'Why should we ever want to say *three* times a day?' came plaintively from Patsy.

'Many time you will be saying it, Memsahib. Every lady in my country retires with stomach trouble to her room. You have to take *dawai*, the medicine dose to be cured. Repeat please, *Teen dafa roz roz*.'

My ambition was to be able to speak the language as well as Sheila who had learnt it from childhood. I had heard her speaking in Hindi to the Prime Minister of Kashmir using the gracious '*ap*' for 'you' instead of the more familiar '*tum*' we used to the servants.

፠   ፠   ፠   ፠

One day after such a lesson Sheila called for me to go shopping, 'not that there is any need to shop here, but it's quite fun,' she said as we set forth through the small back gate which led to the Bund lined with willow trees, the Jhelum flowing by. Roy and Glory came with us on leads. 'Any merchant,' Sheila explained, 'can be summoned to the Residency to display his wares. But I like browsing round the shops to get new ideas for presents. Of course when I personally buy something it means the servants don't get their rake-off, their *dastur* as it is known out here.'

'Doesn't that make it less expensive in the shops?'

'Not really. The shopkeepers add a bit for our benefit.' Sheila went on to tell me that because of the heavy import duty there were few English or foreign goods in the State. For the necessary provisions which were not obtainable locally - and many were not - she ordered at regular intervals bulk stores to be delivered by rail and bus from P. Simms in Bombay. Butter came in one pound tins from Walter Reeves of Madras, wines and spirits from Pondicherry and so on, all delivered from thousands of miles away. The arrival of the mail was always an eagerly awaited daily event. As well as parcels all the way from England, there were the 'crossed bags' (confidential) and the 'un-crossed bags' (non-confidential) for the Secretariat or Dem and myself to deal with.

Apart from the bulk orders, the household managed on local commodities bought in the bazaar. *Basan* was particularly important for softening the water; *ghi*, the white clarified butter was used in cooking. There were the home-grown spices for the making of curry by bashing the ingredients on a stone, this the *mati's* job, and a much used dark unrefined treacle called *gur*. Important too was the linseed crop harvested from the fields and manufactured into the valuable oil which amongst other things was used to treat the walnut furniture which was liable to crack in the dry atmosphere as much as our skins!

On this my first shopping expedition, Sheila and I walked along the pathway skirting the Jhelum river which I had followed in the tortuous valley on the journey up. Here the river was broad and smooth-running and full of craft of all shapes and sizes with a few private houseboats tied up on the opposite bank one of which belonged to Mr Apcar. The river, with its seven wooden bridges on carved trusses, bisected the city of Srinagar. The river wound its way on through the town to a lock into the Dal Lake.

To begin with we passed other large houses standing well back in their gardens along the Bund. Houses soon gave way to small stores displaying the fine arts of Kashmir and here the path became congested with pedestrians and hand carts. The names of the shops were quaint and charming, old world names such as 'Suffering Moses', 'Sunshine Alley', 'Subharna the Worst', and 'My Sainted Aunt'. Equally humorous were the names of the *shikaras*, those gaily curtained and canopied water-taxi gondolas that plied the lakes.

'Suffering Moses' was a particular favourite shop of the British. Sheila and I browsed round their displays of walnut merchandise in the shape of lampstands, nests of tables, bowls, cigarette boxes, small escritoires with sections for letters sold as sets with pen containers and blotting-paper holders. Sheila bought some book-ends with beautifully carved ibex heads for a wedding present to a newly engaged pair. Other shops displayed papier-mâché goods showing the birds of Kashmir, the hoopoes, kingfishers, long-tailed birds of paradise, all beautifully painted in gold leaf in soft pastel colours. I succumbed to a small trinket bowl, one of many purchases to come.

We went on to 'Mahatta', the photographer, and then perhaps the most loved shop of all amongst the ladies, 'Butterfly'. He made underclothes to order, cami-knicks, petticoats, nightgowns, dressing-gowns and negligées in exquisite crêpe-de-chîne or white or pink satin, each garment distinguished by his finely embroidered motif. Finally we dived into a tiny *shafa khana* where the chemist obligingly made up more bottles of oil dosed with sweet smelling essence to splash into our bath water. Sheila suggested I buy a bottle of witch-hazel mixed with rosewater as a moisturizer to smooth daily under make-up, also some colourless salve to apply to lips, at which I at first protested.

'Winter will soon be here,' Sheila insisted. 'You cannot imagine what cold weather is like in Kashmir until you have experienced it, a different cold from anything we have in England or Scotland. If you don't use salve, your lips will become too sore to smile.'

Retracing our steps we let the dogs off the leads to gambol past the Club, beyond the Residency back gate, with its tennis courts and balcony over-looking the river, scene of many fun parties and dances in the future.

When we returned to the Residency we found our purchases had already been delivered and, neatly packed, were awaiting us in the hall. No fuss, no hassle, no trouble. Truly, I thought to myself, this really is a lotus-eating life. What are the snags? A few months later I ran into them.

8
Residents and Bagmen

About a month after my arrival, by which time it was distinctly colder, a return invitation arrived from Mr Apcar, met on my first evening at the Residency. Since then I had quizzed Dem on the origin of the house-boats of Kashmir made so popular by the British. He answered enthusiastically and in some detail as he always liked to do when 'putting me in the picture'.

'The story runs,' Dem said on this occasion, 'that the Kashmir house-boat was first instigated by an Englishman in the last century who had a passion for shooting duck. He decided that rather than living on shore and turning out in the dark of early morning, it would be much more comfortable to live on the spot, so to speak. The boat he had built for himself was reputed to be enormous, complete with dovecote, tower and garden. Attached to it was a smaller house-boat for the kitchen with yet another alongside as servants quarters, all connected by planks. Quite a tricky business serving a four course dinner on a windy night such as this evening,' Dem looked out of the windows at the swaying chenar branches. 'Many are the hilarious tales of bearers falling in with the soup! Mr Apcar does himself well. He brought his own Punjabi cook and personal bearer of long standing with him. The Kashmiri servants do the more lowly work; looked down on by the Punjabis...'

'As Dost Mohammed looks down on what he calls the "scum of Bombay",' I interrupted.

'Quite. Awful hierarchical bigotry in the country born of the caste system. Well done, Evelyn. You're coming on!'

That evening Dem, Sheila, Ronnie and I walked through the back gate leading to the Bund and practically opposite the *ghat* steps to where the Residency *shikara* resplendently awaited us. Six boatmen stood at the ready even for this short journey. A mist had risen on the river and I hugged my new tippet fur close about me as I sank back on downy cushions. In no time Mr Apcar's brightly lit opulent home, as long and white as a battleship, loomed up before us.

On deck we were warmly welcome by our host and ushered into a large drawing-room. We could have been in London. The room had a fitted carpet with expensive looking rugs over; windows were close curtained in velvet; there were chintz fitted sofa covers and incidental chairs tastefully arranged interspersed with antique furniture facing a mantelpiece above a blazing fireplace. On one wall there was a large bookcase stuffed with well thumbed books. Under the carved wooden ceiling hung collectors pictures worth a fortune. I was introduced to the other guests, namely Dr Rawlence, a Srinagar resident and member of the Church Missionary Society in India, and Canons Stokoe and Tyndale-Biscoe both of whom were also Kashmir residents of long standing. Drinks were generously served. The conversation flowed among these old friends. Elegant Mr Apcar with his innate courtly manners warmly drew Ronnie and I into his circle.

The dining-room into which we moved was typically Victorian with much silverware on the long sideboard. Silk swathed overhead lights reflected discreet pools onto a table laden with rose bowls and heavily fretworked sweet dishes. Fleet footed *khitmagars* served piping-hot food. As far as I could see no ladened trays had fallen into the water!

I sat flanked by the delightful Canons who chatted away, sometimes to each other over my head. Canon Stokoe was a rotund red-faced man with silver-grey hair and quizzical wrinkles round humorous eyes. He told me about the British residents in Srinagar: 'my errant flock' he called them with obvious affection. 'They come to Church most Sundays,' he related, 'and they listen attentively enough to my sermons. However I do not think I make much impression upon them spiritually.'

'I am surprised there are so many residents. I always thought the British went home after their time in India?' I questioned.

'Not always by any means, especially not in Kashmir and hill stations such as Murree. Those that stay on are mostly retired army or civil servants, forestry wallahs and the like. Some of the real *koi-hais*, known as "Anglo-Indians" from John Company's days are as dyed-in-the-wool as ourselves! One great attraction is that there is no servant problem here as there is at home. We have become used to being waited on. Those who have been here a long time are looked after by faithful bearers as ancient as they. And, too, living is inexpensive.'

'Yet you still call England home?'

'Of course,' took up Canon Tyndale-Biscoe, 'that's where our families are; that's where our pensions come from. The war in Europe, though, is causing us difficulties.' I knew about that. Since the outbreak, Dem's office had been inundated with messages and distress calls from worried people asking for advice. Due to ships having been attacked at sea, pensions had not arrived on time and some people had run out of money. Should they try and get passages back or should they stay put?

Tyndale-Biscoe was the shorter of the two Canons, a small man who wore a drooping moustache and was famous on three accounts. The first was for having been coxwain of a victorious Cambridge eight in his youth. Secondly for having run for fifty years a missionary school for Brahmin boys and girls in the heart of the Srinagar bazaar. Thirdly for having taught these children to swim so

Prize-giving of C.M.S. Tyndale-Biscoe School
Dem with Canon C Tyndale-Biscoe

well they had achieved high aquatic expertise as could be seen in the school's annual water-sports display when spectacular diving took place from off the city bridges. This was an amazing achievement, for no high-caste Hindu in Kashmir had ever swum from right down the centuries. A father would rather see his only son drown than rescue him himself and so become defiled according to his religion.

The conversation round the table turned from the British poor, who at least could go to the Resident for help and whom the missionaries looked after when they became ill - Dr Rawlence was the most compassionate of men who took the elderly into his hospital free and saw they were nursed to the end - to the local poor who were far worse off. Here Mr Apcar chipped in to tell me how the locals lived in their small boats clustered together in every waterway, branch or cutting with no water supply other than the river for cooking and sanitation. 'Winter especially,' he informed, 'is the time of great hardship when many die of pneumonia, particularly the children and the old. The freezing wind, known as the *banihal*, after which the 9,000 foot high Pass is named, gets into their lungs and gives them hacking coughs as the doctor here will tell you.'

'Indeed,' nodded Dr Rawlence, 'everywhere one goes in the city one hears these sepulchral sounds. To try and keep some warmth in their bodies when outside, the men and women hang small containers called *kangris* from a strap round their necks under their tent-like clothing. It is virtually a fire-pot wherein charcoal glows red hot to warm...'

'And often to scorch,' added Sheila from her end of the table.

'How dangerous!' exclaimed Ronnie.

'Ah,' said Mr Apcar, 'but what is the pain of a burn when you are freezing to death?'

'True,' nodded Canon Tyndale-Biscoe. He went on to say that it looked as if he would be the next to call on the Residency for funds. Apparently since the outbreak of war in Europe money for the Mission, up until then sent out regularly from England, had dried up. 'People have more urgent matters to spend their money on. If things go on this way the school will have to close,' he ended sadly.

'Unthinkable!' declared Dem, and the company started to discuss how money could be raised. Sheila suggested a gala evening next season in the Residency garden with stalls and side shows. Mr Apcar volunteered to give one of his pictures in an auction to tide the mission over, a donation which everyone agreed was a capital idea and one to which the wealthy Princes would contribute.

Dinner over, the party adjourned to the roof-terrace. This was a garden in itself lit with fairy lights over a central flower bed with potted plants stacked the length of the house-boat. Over the way the Bund hummed with movement and flickering lanterns.

Back in the drawing-room the lights were turned low, and Mr Apcar, a great lover of classical music, gave us a concert from his collection of records.

63

I sat back on the sofa sipping crème-de-menthe, listening and watching the others. Sheila had her eyes closed, one dainty foot tapping to the music. The men cupped and tilted their bulbous brandy glasses, and Ronnie smoked Balkan Sobranies to fill the room with their pungent aroma. Both worthy Canons fell asleep. I felt Mr Apcar had abundantly proved his point about being civilized - and, anyway to my knowledge, no gentleman had watered the river!

The following day, Sunday, our Residency party walked the short distance along the Bund to All Saints' Church with its high pitched roof and graceful steeple set in a small luxuriant garden on either side of a winding drive. A flag-pole bearing the St George's emblem flew above the blooms. We sat in a serried rank in the reserved front pew with Dem on the aisle side accessible to read the lesson.

Canon Stokoe delivered an excellent sermon for exactly ten minutes in which he declared himself in ringing tones to be a servant of the Lord. I gathered that even if he were tempted to go on longer than the deemed time, Dem's exaggerated gesture right beneath the pulpit to examine his wrist watch, was blatant enough to halt even the good Canon in his stride.

As the full congregation trooped out into the sunshine I found it hard to believe Canon Stokoe's story against himself that he could make little headway with the residents of Srinagar. Headway or no, they came Sunday after Sunday to enjoy his rousing sermons.

⚜   ⚜   ⚜   ⚜

On another shopping expedition Sheila took me inland from the river past the whitely painted Nedou's Hotel where we stopped to have coffee and meet friends - to 'Hadows' so that I could chose some tapestry. She assured me I would need this work to keep me occupied in the long winter evenings to come. I was beginning to dread this bleak winter I was told about when lips cracked, skin became chapped and it was almost impossible to keep warm unless in bed or huddled before a fire, and indeed so it proved to be. However we did have an escape from it as shall be related.

But first Major Ken Hadow. He was an Englishman who many years previously had set up in Srinagar what was to become a flourishing carpet business. He had discovered that the 'illiterate' Kashmiri was a skilled and varied craftsman who made exquisite carvings, paintings, embroidery, delicate cash-mere shawls, tapestry work - and carpets. As well as the normal woven carpets, for which small children were brought in to work the looms with their quick skilful tiny fingers making the smallest and tightest of knots, Major Hadow saw an opening for the hand stitched carpets and drapes such as I had admired in the Residency dining-room curtains and the round turquoise carpet in the drawing-room.

To begin with - I had had no experience of tapestry work before - Sheila suggested I try my hand with a simple card table cover. The canvas chosen was already prepared with the flower patterns undersewn in the right coloured wools. All I had to do was to fill in the design where indicated with a mixture of petit-point and cross stitch. When I had finished the piece, I would take it back to the Hadow's men who, for a few extra rupees, would stitch in the tedious background in beige.

Going round the factory it was fascinating to watch the men at work. About ten sat on the floor round a rug, each man stitching whirls of coloured pattern in a chainstitch to represent the Kashmir hillsides of wild flowers, the birds and butterflies. Every inch of the cloth was covered in this stitch, and when finished the carpet was lined with beige *dasuti* cloth. I was so intrigued by the process that I then and there ordered a length of bare white flannel to be worked in flowers of varied pinks. After a week or so I called in again and found every inch of the material covered in embroidery. The *darzi* sitting on our verandah at the back, proceeded to make the length up into a dressing-gown. With the pieces left over a shoemaker from the bazaar covered some leather slippers to match. Though the dressing-gown, after serving me well for many years, has long since disintegrated, I still have the pretty slippers. This brings to mind how the same cobbler made me light-weight *chappals* in a variety of shades to match each of my cotton day dresses for summer. In the Indian Army the men and officers wore a heavyweight studded version of these open-toed sandals, excellent for mountain warfare. The leather was smartly mirror-polished for parade.

Our *darzi* sat as regularly on the back verandah by day as did the *chowkidar* by night. He sat cross-legged on a rug before his ancient hand-driven sewing machine which had 'Singer' written in Persian lettering across its width. All day long the oiled machine purred busily to and fro, a soothing sound to which I fell asleep in the afternoons when resting from one evening's marathon to the next. The *darzi* was permanently employed at the Residency. There was always work for him to do from making new curtains, repairing the household linen, sewing shirts for the men, turning out new scarlet uniforms for the *chaprassis*, not to mention dresses for the *burra* Mem and the Miss-sahibs copied out of Vogue. As the weather turned colder he made warm shirts for Ronnie of fine pashmina wool spun from the under-hair of goats, and short-sleeved spencers of the same wool for me. He also made me some long sleeved woollen evening dresses of which I had come out unprepared. These were often made with matching boleros for extra warmth, so cold did the Residency become. It may have had modern plumbing but it had no central heating of any sort.

Invariably there was something of interest going on in the deep back verandahs or in the square entrance hall where the *farash* footmen hung about with the colourful *chaprassis* waiting for the next message to be taken or received, but most interesting of all to me were the bagmen, as the itinerant merchants were called. Most visited regularly once or twice a year and were welcomed as old friends. They came great distances on foot in yak and mule caravans carrying their goods. They were fed and put up in the servants quarters.

'*China-man agaya,* Memsahib,' de Mello would announce with beaming face. Once it was during a dinner party.

'Oh, do let's see what he brings!' the ladies exclaimed; and after the meal the hall floor would be littered with his goods to examine and admire.

The Chinaman brought underwear for us, and for the men silk pyjamas with dragons embroidered on the pockets. There were fine cross-stitched tray and tea cloths with small napkins to match, lacquer tea sets with red and gold painting on the insides, and little cups and saucers with matching spoons just the right size for after-dinner coffee. With these went black lacquer trays, fruit plates and finger bowls. There were prettily painted china soup bowls with their matching lids, saucers, and curving spoons from which to choose a set of eight. Also displayed were exquisite ornaments both in white and green jade which Ronnie and I held admiringly but could never afford even though they were at bargain prices. The Chinaman encouraged us to finger his goods as much as we liked and to drape his satins and gossamer materials over chairs and balustrades to see the effect. Once we had made our purchases he had everything neatly folded and packed up into his bags in a jiffy.

These roving Chinamen would stay in India a year, sometimes two, while travelling round a favourite beat of 'regulars' with the *chittis* of recommendation we always gave him, until he had sold all his wares. Then he would travel back the long way 'over the top of the world' following the silk route to China to replenish his stocks for the next trip. It was quite a thing to welcome back a familiar Chinaman after his long absences. But would there be a next time?

'What happen to poor China-man now, Master, Missee?' I remember our favourite bagman expressing, his wrinkled face a study of woe. 'Big war stop China-man to come back. Fan Lo face ruin!'

'You must come back, Fan Lo; what would we do for presents without you? Take this *chitti* and go to Hong Kong, that's British, and then you can return.'

He got to Hong Kong (so the servants informed) and was allowed into the Colony with all his recommendations from the Memsahibs of India, and there he was caught by the war. He never came back.

☙   ☙   ☙   ☙

66

Always of great interest to the men particularly was the carpet man who came to display his shimmering rugs and camel-bags which he spread out in the hall. He too carried his heavy loads by mule-pack and yak over the mountain passes and through the dusty deserts, though in a more westerly direction than the Chinaman's route. He brought intricately patterned brightly coloured saddle-bags with their long tasselled fringes from Shiraz in Southern Persia, and superbly ornate silk prayer-mats from Kashan in Iran; the loosely knitted fringed rugs from Kazakh of longer pile; rugs from the Caucasus; Bokhara carpets of magenta or puce, and the many less expensive and coarser woven ones of blues, green and browns from Kula, Afghanistan and Baluchistan. These carpets once again reflected the Persian love of flowers, of massed roses and carnations, of hunting scenes and exotic lotuses which showed the Chinese influence.

The 'good' rugs were not cheap even then, though at prices low compared to now-a-days, and much haggling went on until an agreement was struck. Dem examined them on the reverse side for the number of stitches to the inch and the closeness of knots. The men even tested for fastness of dyes by immersion into hot water before being satisfied.

When the weather turned cold, the bagman we females clustered round was the furrier. Those were the days when there was no shortage of game in India. The jungles, countryside and mountains were rife with wild animals. Villagers in those days were unarmed, and the jungles were carefully preserved and watched over by forestry men and experts such as Colonel Jim Corbett of tiger fame who made sure the jungles were closed in the breeding seasons, the numbers shot monitored. He was a man with a deep love for all birds and beasts, an expert shot himself who studied their habitat and devoted his life particularly to tiger preservation. Jim Corbett had a mission. He was a brave man who went out on foot to track down beasts who were terrorizing villagers, the tiger having through old age or some disability become a man-eater.

We women in the Residency already had furs. I had brought out with me my heavy beaver-lamb full length coat my father had given me for my last birthday. Ronnie had a moth-eaten astrakhan which had belonged to her mother, and Sheila had a panther skin coat she had shot in Central India herself. But we were all agreed that if we were going to survive in the draughty Residency in the next two months to come, when we were required to change into evening dress every single night, we needed a fur tippet to clutch around necks.

With no shortage in Kashmir, the furrier came to display a good selection of wolf and fox, but on being shown the sandy-red furred Kashmir snow-lynx, we all three unanimously voted for that. The animal was prized and rare because he lived in inaccessible mountain country in the great heights and was extremely difficult to spot so that most were left undetected and undisturbed. Silkily longhaired and beautifully warm, the skins of our choice were made up into capes and lined with satin with a small pocket inside to hold compact and handkerchief. I wore mine for the first time to Mr Apcar's dinner party.

9
Picnic to Nishat Bagh

One morning not long after my arrival, when there had been a flurry of work for me to do for Dem, and I was just beginning to get the hang of what my varied job entailed, a young man walked into the dining room when we were breakfasting at the round table in the bay window. He was welcomed by the family, by Ronnie and also by de Mello. It was obvious that he had been up here several times before.

He was Sheila's younger brother, Stuart, come to stay for what they called ten days 'casual' leave from his regiment stationed in Risalpur in the North West Frontier Province not far from Peshawar. I had known he was due to arrive, but not that early! I reckoned he must have risen in the dark to have come all the way from Risalpur in time for breakfast. I soon learnt that he was as early a riser as was his elder brother Keith who liked to ride before breakfast, and declared *that* to be the best part of the day which sluggerbeds missed - their loss! Consequently it was also 'early to bed' with the brothers as I had found out in Austria.

I had been in a ski-ing party got up by Dem and Sheila which had included Keith, on leave from India, and Derek Anderson, a cousin, another unmarried man. With these two escorts I had a whale of a time though there had been dark overtones when Black Shirts carrying lighted torches and Nazi banners had swept down the mountain slopes to be greeted by the apparently enthusiastic townsfolk of Kitzbühel. Since then Keith had married Joan, the daughter of the Governor of Assam. Keith was also, like Dem, in the Political and by a happy fluke was posted to Gilgit where his wife and baby daughter joined him. They were due to visit the Residency later in the year.

But this young man, though as good looking as were his brother and sister, bore little resemblance to either. Aged thirty-one he was now a Captain, a dashing-looking cavalryman who commanded a mounted troop in his unit. He had dark auburn wavy hair and a moustache to match. He wore the wide flannel trousers of the day with a light-coloured somewhat battered looking tweed jacket from which a regimental tie floated. On his feet were the thick soled desert boots.

I took this much in as he was being greeted by his family. He then came up to shake hands, and to give me a straight look from very blue eyes. I imagined that he had heard about me - the girl who was coming out to India to be Dem's PA and to help Sheila - as I had heard about him, the kid brother who was a lover of nature from butterflies to big game who spent as much time as he could in the jungle or trekking in the mountains, a keen shot and a fine horseman having had six month's training at the Saugor Cavalry School. This had led him to go in for cross-country and show jumping competitions and polo. I had heard that he had a girl in England to whom he was privately engaged, and that he had recently taken leave to fly home to stay with her. Both sets of parents (Sheila's father and mother were in Malta and shortly to be under siege) were said to be delighted with the match. Why then, with the advent of war and all parents pressing them, had they not married or at least become officially engaged? In the days that followed our introduction I would not have dreamed of asking him. I found him good mannered, quiet and extremely reserved.

A few days later, after having been run off my feet with all my duties, Dem came up with the suggestion that Ronnie and I took a day off to go and see the famous Moghul gardens. 'Stuart knows them well,' he said, 'he'll show you round.'

'Good idea,' exclaimed Sheila, 'wear your slacks for the ride and take a warm jumper. I'll fix a picnic with de Souza.' In the event Ronnie withdrew as Glory's time was drawing near. Thus Stuart was lumbered with me alone for a whole day, a time that to my mind was bound to be sticky with him pining for his girl friend in England! However that was no business of mine. I was longing to see the gardens of 'Pale hands I loved' fame, and, sticky or no, I was going to enjoy myself. We set forth with picnic basket and rugs by the back gate to the *ghat* steps.

The Residency *shikara*, already familiar to me with its six boatmen, is best described as a privately owned gondola a great deal more resplendent than the smaller taxi-*shikaras* which plied their hire in the lakes. Our long craft was painted in gold and green and it had curtains tied back at four corners, curtains which could be pulled right round to ensure complete privacy if wanted. Overhead the awnings were canopied in scarlet and yellow.

'I feel like something out of Omar Khayyam,' I said as I sank back on brightly coloured cushioned seats as wide as a bed while the boatmen in their scarlet liveries propelled the craft out to mid stream with long-handled paddles. 'I gather you already know Kashmir?'

'Pretty well. I've been up for the ski-ing in Gulmarg and into camp for the fishing. I was once in a houseboat in the hot weather. That was before Dem became Resident. I've stayed with them in Mount Abu and for various shooting camps in the CP at Christmas, but never done it in style like this!'

I nodded. It was a very stylish progress as once in midstream our pace increased, the boatmen sending us along smoothly in effortless strokes, and skilfully steering the long boat past other craft.

'They say the river is filthy, but it doesn't look all that dirty,' I observed,' as I dangled my hand in the water.

'Clean enough. What the eye doesn't see...'

'Sheila doesn't think so. She's very particular.'

'Quite right to be. She's had dysentery. You should look out too as a newcomer.'

'What about Dem?'

'Oh, he's cast iron!'

We lapsed into silence. In any case there was no need for chatter, there was so much to observe as we swept on under one of the picturesque wooden bridges from where fair-skinned but extremely grubby urchins wearing their vividly embroidered Kashmir caps waved to us. On either side of the river numerous lesser canals branched off and intersected each other in a mass of waterways packed with the house-boats of the population. We passed rickety looking houses built of small red bricks and woodwork, with tiers of carved wooden balconies which jutted crazily out over the water, their prettily carved lattice-work windows half covered with wild geranium plants now turning scarlet.

A mosque with kerosene tin roof glinted in the sun as we swept by. Next came into view a temple built of stone, topped with hanging bells, tall above the stacked houses. Covered barges and great long grain boats rested tethered to banks shaded by russet-brown wild cherry and apricot trees. The smell of frying mustard oil with whiffs of stinking refuse reached me in hot waves, and always before us, as we proceeded, high above the old city and never entirely hidden, glistened the everlasting mountains. There they were, beckoning us on towards the lakes, last winter's old snow freshly tipped by a new fall to foretell the imminent arrival of winter.

We came to the Dal *darwaza*, the lock gate connecting the Jhelum River with the Dal Lake. Our *shikara* waited behind the wooden gates which regulated the different water levels. Then we floated out to a widening channel to emerge into the open lake itself. Here the boatmen standing behind us paddled more strongly to push the boat through tightly packed patches of lotus plants.

'You should see it when the lotus is flowering,' my companion said.

'That's what they all say: wait for spring, wait for summer. My stock answer to this is it's good enough for me now!'

Before us was indeed a lovely sight, oft named one of the wonders of the world. On our right rose the Takht-i-Suleiman hill with its little Hindu temple gracefully atop. Way over to the east lay the Shalimar gardens, that 'abode of love', and two miles short of it lay the Nishat Bagh, the 'garden of bliss' or 'gladness' reputed to be at its best in autumn. It was for this garden we were heading, still quite a paddle away. On the other shore lay the Nasim or Naghim Bagh, the 'garden of breezes' so called for its eastern aspect. Here was the earliest of the gardens with chenars planted in Shah Jehan's time. Above this garden lay, on an isolated hill, the Hari Parbat fort built by Akbar, still used as a prison and said to be a fearful place.

The Dal Lake was virtually a series of lakes, divided by bunds and small islands, in the centre of the vast plain ringed by foothills and backed by the white capped ranges. On that peerless warm autumn day the reflections of the mountains in the still water were so clear, so true, it was like looking into a shining mirror which so faithfully reproduced the scene one could not tell which was real, which reflected. The whole Vale was ablaze with autumn tints, the lake giving the effect of a double radiance of colours. The poplars, the crab apples and cherries, the hazel and walnut trees vied with one another in the brilliance of their yellows, golden-browns, reds and burnished coppers, while the leaves of the willows fluttered down in silvery droves by the gently lapping water's edge.

'That's Haramokh, nearly 17,000 feet high,' Stuart pointed ahead at the most conspicuous peak. 'Twenty-four miles distant yet it feels as if one only has to stretch out a hand to touch it, don't you think? To the west over there is the Khagan range, seventy miles away.'

'I've heard Kashmir likened to Switzerland which I know well having spent some summers there, but I don't agree with the comparison. The valleys I remember are narrow compared to the length and breadth of this plain, and as for the mountains.... well these stupendous ones dwarf the highest in the Alps.'

'True. Mont Blanc a pimple! Nor any lakes this size.' I turned to look at Sheila's brother who knew the names of the mountains and ranges around us. His eyes scanned the far horizons as naval men's did, eyes attuned to wide open spaces. I knew he had trekked up into the mountains alone except for his bearer, and that he had walked the paths up to Kathmandu in Nepal to stay at the Residency there, and also to Gyantze in Tibet; both lands then without roads and both closed countries for which permits had first to be obtained. I thought he was a bit of a loner, a self-contained reticent man, one difficult if not impossible to get to know. He seemed to me the total opposite of what in the army were known as 'poodle fakers'. Small talk was obviously not in his line, and anyway talk seemed superfluous as our *shikara* glided on over the glassy surface now that we had left the patches of lotus leaves far behind.

We passed other humbler *shikaras* piled with produce and wood, women squatting in the prows, old men feathering and steering as they paddled. On one narrow boat a tall Kashmiri wearing the usual skull cap, stood motionless in the bow of his skiff; one hand held poised a three-pronged spear, while the other slowly propelled the boat along. Suddenly, as we watched, he struck and swiftly withdrew from the water a small wriggling fish.

Now we were well out in the open lake. On the far shore were anchored a string of tall house-boats looking like Noah's Arks with their top decks awningless, their windows shuttered at this late time of year. Each had individual names such as 'Christmas Treat', 'Royal George' or 'Water Beetle'. These house-boats were booked up for the summers from year to year by the many who came up regularly in the hot weather on leave. For the taxi *shikaras*, often secluded in their drawn curtains, the Kashmiris once again indulged their sense-of-humour and their pulling-the-legs of the British by devising such names as

'Whoopee', 'Love-in-the-Mist', 'Skylark' and 'Love-lies-Bleeding'!
Nearing the far shore where the mountains towered close above the water, we passed many islands, one large, one stately with chenar trees. The smaller islands were in fact artificial. They gave the appearance of floating in the blue sky, and were man-made from weeds cut from the lake and bound together to form base rafts. Then, with mud scooped out from the canals and backwaters, the islands were covered with harvested lotus leaves to make manure. On this rich soil grew prolific crops of leguminous vegetables from potatoes, melons, cucumbers and so on, also fodder for the animals cooped up in huts and in the ground floors of farm houses. The islands were moored by staking with long willow poles, and they could be towed to change position when convenient. Every bit of extra land was of immense value to the Kashmiri farmer who cultivated the little islands and whatever valuable strips of ground he could acquire between lake and mountain.

❦   ❦   ❦   ❦

By a bund we glided into an inner lake and under a bridge where brilliant dragonflies darted over the water; iridescent blue kingfishers, larger than any I had seen in England, flashed to and fro from holes in the banks. Before us came into view a small pink pavilion by the landing stage of the Nishat Bagh, the largest of the famous Moghul gardens and perhaps the most spectacular in its setting with the rocky mountain rising steeply behind to give the impression of hanging over the garden. Bisecting the garden from top to bottom ran a mountain stream into the lake.

We jumped out, glad to stretch legs after the two hour paddle. Looking about me I saw that the garden was built in the form of a series of stone terraces, each one, so Stuart informed me for the signs of the zodiac. Stone steps led beside the central water-course. Up we went across short expanses of scruffy grass to the next rise of steps past basins filled with jutting fountains and small waterfalls with only a trickle of water now running from its source in the far glaciers. This small stream bubbled its way down under white marble seats bordered by formal beds of zinnias and a few bushes of roses set in the sparse grass. The flower beds were flanked by an avenue of tall chenars clothed in their rich autumn foliage of scarlets and golds.

On reaching the topmost terrace we turned to lean on the wall and gaze down at the steep garden, and the multicoloured lake before with the mountains clear in the distance beyond the smokey haze of Srinagar. Not only was I short of breath after the climb, but the view was enough to take one's breath away!

I noticed Stuart looking at me quizzically. 'Sitting at a typewriter and doing the flowers,' he observed patronizingly, 'isn't going to get you into training for trekking up to Gulmarg let alone Gilgit. I'll give you a game of tennis

Nishat Bagh

73

or two while I'm up here if you like. You see that col over there to the East,' he pointed before I had time to protest that I played tennis with his brother-in-law and was pretty fit, thank-you, 'it is in the Pir Panjal range which one goes over to get to Jammu and Sialkot. There's a tunnel at the summit. It's called the Banihal.'

'It doesn't look as if a road could get up that craggy steepness,' I declared.

'Fairly hair-raising. Are you car sick?'

'I survived the journey up from Murree.'

'Oh, the Banihal is *far* worse than the Murree road which remains open in winter unless there's a landslide. The Banihal Pass is closed annually by snow.'

The twenty foot top terrace upon which we stood ran the full width of the garden with *zenanas*, or women's quarters, built like gazebos, at either end. 'In them,' it was my turn to inform, Sheila having told me something of the history of the ancient garden we were to visit, 'the Moghul ladies sat in the open balconies which faced in three directions, to admire the views and watch the fountains playing on the roses.'

I had also read a book in the Residency shelves on the Moghul Emperors and learnt that they used to sit in their pavilions in the lower terraces with their nobles, their eunuchs and sycophants ready at hand to jump to their slightest wish. Here they, like their womenfolk, enjoyed the peace of the beautiful setting with the garden planted with trees to give them shade, the stream channelled so that they could listen to the soft cool sound of splashing water which kept the grass green, the bedded flowers bright, and the roses fresh even in the parched heat of summer.

Here was a master-piece of a garden designed by Shah Jehan out of his love for his chaste queen Mumtaz Mahal. The rectangular shape was classic in its simplicity. The pattern of the beds and canals inspired musicians to compose songs, poets to write sonnets, and craftsmen to design the carpets of Persia. The Emperors of old so loved these water gardens that often they could not tear themselves away and stayed on till the passes were blocked with snow and had to be dug out before they could leave. They called the Vale the 'pearl of Hind', and Indians still say no one who has loved Kashmir can be quite whole again 'for its beauty steals the heart'. Looking down on the Nishat Bagh that day I could see why, and it is true that it too stole my heart so that I wrote about it, and went back and found it as beautiful as ever in its setting.

'I like the geometrical pattern of the canals', Stuart with an engineer's eye, appreciated as we strolled down to choose a picnic spot on a grassy bank by the water. I clapped hands to draw the attention of the boatmen to bring our lunch. They came with the rugs and baskets and then sat some little distance away chatting amongst themselves.

'Does the Kashmiri appreciate the beauty of his land?' I wondered.

'I shouldn't think so; too busy scraping a living. If the farmers have a bad harvest, or the tourists are few as they are bound to be with this war, the population faces starvation in winter.'

Pondering on this I unpacked the hamper and we tucked in. I could see only one other party in the Nishat Bagh on that day late in the season, a family group of locals. The men squatted down in a circle talking together while the women sat apart, just as royalty of old had done in the same garden, while watching their children playing with the water. The women were strikingly good-looking, fair skinned, their blue eyes underscored with black making them look huge. They wore their hair in thin plaits hanging long over their tent-like dresses. From the lobes of their ears hung earrings as ornate as candelabras, and they jingled with silver jewellery as they walked with superb carriage and grace.

I was drinking my coffee and idly watching the family group when I was amazed to see a mouse tottering across the grass, like a drunken old man, in our direction. Stuart saw it at the same moment and put his hand up to indicate that I remain still. I thought the mouse must be damaged as I watched it stumbling blindly on. Then it came to me that it was dazed by fear, for behind it and following ruthlessly its curving way, appeared a snake. Watching the drama, I too felt paralysed. Then Stuart in one deft movement caught up a beer bottle and, leaping to his feet, despatched the snake with a well-aimed blow. The mouse, instantly recovering, scuttled off into the safety of some bushes.

I hid my unease. I felt the incident had brought a cloud to darken the peerless day. We were in a Garden of Eden where snakes timelessly and inevitably chased their prey. What would happen to the beautiful land of Kashmir when the British, who had ruled benevolently and who had kept the peace between the factions for so long, went? Would these royal gardens be fought over, the temples and mosques, pavilions and gazebos be destroyed, the handsome, humorous inhabitants and their lovely children be killed and maimed?

At least, I comforted myself looking again across the lake, nothing man did could destroy the beauty of the vast mountainous range of the Himalayas.

10
Ronnie and the Puppies

Glory and Roy had their own 'bearer'. He was a low caste Kashmiri, the lowest of the low, the poorest and the worst paid. They were known as sweepers, and sometimes *bhangis* or *mehtars* the latter Urdu for a prince, a tongue-in-cheek name for those whose plight Mahatma Gandhi brought to the public eye, as untouchables. They emptied the night soil buckets, were the cleaners of outside places, swept the roads and the paths with twig brooms. They were a responsible, kindly, long-suffering people, an indispensable part of the life in India - and they looked after the sahib's dogs. Our sweeper saw to the dog's food under Ronnie's supervision, brushed and groomed their coats until they shone and every curly hair was combed out like a baby's; moreover he loved the dogs and they him. He slept in the dog room downstairs, all three on identical charpoys, the Indian string-woven beds.

The sweeper exercised his charges several times a day. In between they could roam at will in the large garden. The guards at the lodges were instructed to see that they did not get out into the bazaar to mix with the common pi-dogs and pick up horrible diseases. But Roy was too smart for the guards, his instincts too great, and frequently he found routes by which to escape and mix with attractive - to him - bitches to show that he was not in the least inhibited by his high breeding.

A month before we were due to leave for the plains, when the whole Residency staff, including the Office, servants, Surgeon, Assistant Resident and so on, moved down to Sialkot for four winter months leaving the Residency shuttered, and cold under dust sheets in the care of the *chowkidars*, Glory produced her litter of puppies, and there was a rabies scare.

There were six puppies, all blonde, squirming, misty eyed and adorable. Ronnie, in at the accouchement, moved her room downstairs to be with them day and night. The sweeper, with Roy, was banished to an out-house. Ronnie was kept constantly busy feeding the puppies by hand as Glory did not have enough milk for all. The dog-ward was kept to an even temperature with oil heaters. The whole place, and indeed much of the Residency, smelt of TCP which Ronnie used externally and also internally for the puppies as a de-wormer. She was in her element, humming about her work, eyes glinting happily, cigarette ash dropping everywhere as she dashed in and out of the kitchen with her hands full of little bowls. We thought she was being rather over-particular until one day in an absolute downpour Patsy rushed into the Residency white to the gills, trembling, and dripping with rain.

Ronnie on house-boat, Dal Lake, Srinagar

'Michael has been bitten by a mad dog!' she wailed, water trickling down her neck from sodden fair ringlets, 'he's covered in blood!'

'Where is he? How did it happen?' we gasped while leaping to our feet in the drawing-room.

'Someone's taken him off to hospital. We were out walking on the Bund beyond the Club, and, and, this slobbering beast attacked him....' she faltered. She collapsed into a chair.

'Get the memsahib a brandy,' Dem ordered de Mello who was standing gawping in the doorway.

She gulped some down and we all piled into the Vauxhall and were driven at break-neck speed to the Nursing Home where Michael was just being put to bed after having seven stitches sewn into his face. He looked ghastly.

We ourselves were so shocked at the incident that it was brandies all round when we got back to the Residency. Patsy was put up for the night in a spare room. Captain Ledgard arrived to tell Patsy she must go on the morrow to the hospital to have her first injection. 'The police managed to shoot the dog,' he informed. 'The corpse has been sent off to the Pasteur Institute at Kasauli for rabies tests, but in the circumstances I'm not having anyone taking risks while waiting for the results to come through.'

Patsy practically lived at the Nursing Home until Michael was allowed back. Both husband and wife had to have the anti-rabies injections every day for fourteen days into the skin of the abdominal stomach wall. The treatment was uncomfortable, caused some swelling, bruising and local tenderness and left the couple sore, but that was little enough discomfort compared to the fear and risk of the dread mad-water-wish death from rabies. Patsy, though not actually bitten had had flecks of saliva blown onto her in the melee of shouts and screams in the downpour as the dog leapt to attack Michael, a scene which haunted her for a long time. On his return home Michael came to see us in a terribly nervy state. He looked gaunter than ever, the red scars when unbandaged showing up hideously livid.

So it was a welcome diversion when the Shipton expedition, on passing through Srinagar on their way down from K2 - at over 28,000 feet the second highest peak in the world - came to stay at the Residency. Scott Russell and Dr Fountain were with Eric Shipton, the latter an attractive fair-haired slim young man. (Beatrice Weir, a friend of mine, a lovely girl with long dark hair, who together with her widowed sister Joan-Mary, bearing twins to be, often came to the Residency, and fell head-over-heels in love with Eric, whom she had met on the expedition's way up. It was not to be and she married an officer in the Gurkhas and lived happily ever after to become the mother of Joanna Lumley.)

Blackened by the mountain sun as the men were, to begin with they also appeared remote and withdrawn. Certainly when questioned they had little to say about their adventures. I put the monosyllabic answers down to their having been away from civilization for a year, and wondered how long it would take them to adjust. They knew little of what had been happening in the world and asked for information rather than giving it.

'Well, yes, we succeeded in our mission of surveying the Karakorams. No, we did not get to the summit of K2 nor expected to,' Dr Fountain in the end vouchsafed.

'We curtailed the expedition when we heard that war had broken out. We've come down in a hurry to join up,' Eric Shipton explained their unexpected re-appearance.

'Don't want to miss out.' Scott Russell added.

'No danger of that,' Sheila assured, 'you wouldn't know there was a war on up here. Nor in England where they are calling it a 'phoney' war, so it seems'.

'A Division has been sent from India to Egypt, another to Malaya. You chaps can take your choice,' Dem told them. 'I guarantee plenty of fighting ahead. I only wish I were your age myself....'

꽃   꽃   꽃   꽃

By the beginning of December it had turned bitterly cold in Srinagar. The glory of the autumn tints had vanished, leaves faded and fallen, the grass brown and burnt-looking with the temperature at nights standing at 16° degrees of frost and worse expected. As well as no central heating in the Residency the electricity system was dim and liable to break down at any moment if overloaded. Every grate in the house blazed with log fires. In the evenings we sat in a small circle as close as we could get to the roaring drawing-room hearth. With coal scarce the sweepers made *golis*, which looked like cannon balls, from coal and charcoal dust kneaded together with oil and cow dung. The result gave out a not unpleasant farmyard smell. The *golis* glowed red hot and kept in the heat while the dry logs burnt quickly and constantly needed to be replenished. Whisky-mac was the drink of the evening, a most warming concoction of a tot of whisky poured on top of half a glass of ginger wine.

We three women with our long sleeved woollen evening dresses covering spencers and warm 'bloomer' knickers, our silk clad legs encased in Gilgit boots which were made of padded felt and came up to the knees (the leather soles were thick like a soft platform) found that even with fur tippets as well we were still cold. Especially was it cold in the dining-room as the raw wind whistled down the valleys, rattled the windows, and draughted under doors to lift the rugs on the floors in billowing gusts. I remember seeing one rug actually taking off!

The servants wore poshteen coats made from goat skin with the hair inwards. The sleeves of these coats of the Frontier and Afghanistan were so long they covered the hands and could be used as a muff. The staff were issued with extra rations and fuel for their *godown* fires around which they sat huddled at nights, the men sucking their long pipes or passing round the *hookah* while swapping yarns.

My Hadow's dressing-gown, though of a flannel base, was nothing like warm enough for this cold, and I with the others, men and women alike, had purchased the *choga* coat worn habitually by the men of Gilgit. These were made from a soft but strong cloth woven from sheep's wool, and were full length down to the ankles with short slits at the sides. They were brightly embroidered in coloured silks round hem and wrists. The men's *chogas* with their deep side pockets, were in rich brown, while we ladies chose the cream ones held together across the chest by tasselled silken cords.

Outside the distant mountains took on an ever deepening mauve, and a great silence engulfed the countryside as snow-flakes began to fall. An icy greyness closed in to take possession of the Vale. Men shuffled past on the Bund wrapped in padded coats and blankets, their hands and feet blue and numbed with cold. Shawls were hugged over heads so that it was not possible to tell who was young or old. All one could see of the muffled ghosts was their breath flowing like smoke from the folds. It was time to leave and quickly lest we too became locked in like the Moghul Emperors of old.

ᛘ   ᛘ   ᛘ   ᛘ

The day dawned fine and windless. Fresh snow sparkled in the sun where it had fallen softly overnight. The road over the Banihal Pass was declared to be clear of drifts. Our large party was divided between several cars and lorries. Dem and Sheila set forth early in the Vauxhall, flag flying, Hassan-ud-Din at the wheel; their aim was to arrive in Sialkot in the plains soon after the servants in their lorries. Ronnie and I, the two dogs and the puppies, followed in the Ford shooting-brake at a much more leisurely pace. Ram Singh, a very experienced Sikh, was our chauffeur. Our own lorry with our luggage, our bedding, cooking pots and food for ourselves and the dogs, followed with the sweeper and a bearer.

This small convoy was forced to stop frequently to see to the puppies squealing in a large box in the back of the brake. The rug, with which we endeavoured to keep them warmly covered - there being no heaters in cars in those days and the Pass was a high one - was constantly dislodged by the puppies who played with it and tore at it with their sharp little teeth as they growled and fell over one another in exuberant play.

After leaving the plain with the straight poplar lined road, the way began a steady zig-zag upwards, the bends occurring in ever increasing frequency the higher we progressed. Here the brake proved too long to get round the bends in one go on the steepest gradients. Trying again, with Ronnie and I hanging onto our seats (no seat belts either!) Ram Singh took us sickeningly close to a slippery *khud* drop with no parapet wall, and then reversed even more dangerously near to a crumbling precipitous edge with a thousand foot drop directly beneath us, before accelerating, foot flat down to grind upwards, puppies falling about in every direction. Fortunately there was little traffic coming the other way, and those that did, having spied us from far above, gave a blast from their horns in warning. Even so it was sheer murder as both cars ground to a halt, and Ram Singh inched our way past as near as he dared without scraping the other car who appeared to be tottering on the edge.

To add to the general confusion in the brake of squealing puppies, Roy was sick in the back seat. He was already in bad odour with Ronnie for having disdainfully lifted his leg on the puppies as we were about to embark. We carried on, I holding a handkerchief to my nose and feeling queasy for the first time. I assured myself it was *not* from car sickness.

On the first flat part at the summit before entering the tunnel, we stopped to clean up the car. Ram Singh got out and walked away in lordly manner making it quite clear he was of too high a caste to demean himself by taking part in the proceedings. There was no sighting of the lorry following with the sweeper, and I must confess that I chickened out too and left the smelly task to Ronnie.

Walking away from the car I took great gulps of peerless cold fresh air. Round a bend I stood gazing at the magnificent scenery at the summit of the Banihal Pass. I was at the lowest point in the great Pir Panjal range standing at 9,000 feet in the Col. On either side of me towered range upon range of icy jagged peaks and great snow-clad mountains as far as the eye could see for mile after mile against a high brilliant blue sky dotted with sentinel cotton-wool clouds. It was an exhilarating and breath-taking scene with the only living thing in sight two lammergeyers floating and wheeling further down. The altitude gave me a feeling of being on the point of penetrating the distances to limitless 'forevers', to horizons beyond where other worlds existed unknown to humanity, where Infinity reigned. It was easy to believe in God up there, easy to understand what motivated the mystics, those holy men of the mountains who sat in caves clad only in a loin-cloth in temperatures such as this, bearded skinny men who barely ate and who could send telepathic messages received across the oceans in a jiffy.

Ronnie called me back to earth, and we drove on through the short one-way tunnel and out to where snow was banked high on either side of the road. The descent over the other side seemed just as steep and tortuous as the climb, but we had not far to go. Still high up the Pass we reached our scheduled stop for the night at the hamlet of Kud. The Dak bungalow here consisted - as most Dak bungalows did - of a central room for meals, and two bedrooms each with a concrete floored bathroom consisting of a tin tub and commode. As the other bedroom was already occupied, Ronnie and I had to share. All the room consisted of was two charpoy beds, bare of mattresses or coverings, a rickety table and two chairs. The wooden floor was rugless and looked none too clean. We had not even a piece of soap or a towel to dry our hands on, but we were not too concerned when the *chowkidar* showed us in. Our lorry was on the way with our bedding rolls, food, kitchen utensils and everything we needed. The servants would be put up in the *godowns* and would cook our evening meal in the Dak bungalow kitchen. The *chowkidar* in charge was not required to provide provisions or servants. He was there virtually only to receive the payment.

We busied ourselves by ensconcing the puppies in the bedroom and unloading the car. Then we waited and waited. We got hungrier and hungrier, having had nothing to eat except a light sandwich lunch since our early breakfast ten hours before.

'What has happened to the lorry, Ram Singh?' We called our driver in.

'*Malum nahin* Miss-sahib,' he gesticulated non-committedly. Ronnie told him to go out and look for it. He returned shrugging his shoulders. Still no sign of it and it was getting dark.

'Perhaps it's gone over the *khud*, Ram Singh?' I suggested ghoulishly.

'Very likely, Miss-sahib, with that fool of a Muslim driver at the wheel!' came the scathing reply.

The distinctly grubby *chowkidar* produced tea for our evening meal which we drank from our coffee mugs and finished the remains of our picnic down to the last crumb. Prudently Ronnie had brought one tin of Cow and Gate for the puppies and some meat for the dogs, all of which was lapped up greedily by the puppies and wolfed down by Glory and Roy while we looked on.

It was the most uncomfortable night I had yet spent in India. We were still high up on the mountain and it was bitterly cold. We lay fully dressed under our fur coats on the bare charpoys which we took the precaution of sprinkling liberally with the dogs' Keating's Powder. Right through the night we fed the puppies every four hours which at least helped to pass the time. They seemed not to need any sleep, full of beans and up to every sort of antic as they were in the bare room pulling and tearing at their rug in squealing delight.

At one point Ronnie, fearful that the runt of the litter would catch her death of cold took her into bed with her. Although smaller than the others she had great character and was the most mischievous of them all. From that night on we called her Pickles. The others were named Simon, Medlar, Gunner, Benju, and Blondi all 'of Mintiker' with a long list of antecedents in the Kennel Club of Great Britain where they had duly been recorded.

We must have slept a bit for we awoke cold and stiff to find it was daylight. By now ravenous, we had more tea from the *chowkidar* who also produced a boiled egg each, and decided to press on as soon as we could as there was still no sign of the lorry. The road curved sharply down the mountain through forests of fir trees and on to the lower passes of the Chenab Valley. We stripped as we went. First we shed our fur coats and then jumpers as we descended into the haze of the plains.

In no time we passed through Jammu, the red and white stone capital of Kashmir where Sir Hari Singh had his winter palace. For some reason lost in days long gone by, the Resident had chosen to have his winter abode fourteen miles further on from here in the military cantonment of Sialkot over the border of the Princely State into the British India of the Punjab, governed directly by the Viceroy in Delhi. Sialkot had a pleasant sunny and temperate climate in winter, but was appallingly hot in summer. It was said that the only compensation for being stationed in this red hot 'Aldershot' was the knowledge that within a few hours one could reach the blessed coolth of Kashmir.

To Ronnie and myself, after the rigours of Srinagar in December it already seemed like a heat wave as Ram Singh drove fast along the straight road, his hand almost permanently on the horn. This wide ancient Grand Trunk Road of Moghul and Kipling fame which led on to Lahore and ran the whole way across India to Delhi and Calcutta, was tarmacadamed only in the centre. The verges were thick with white dust. Not unnaturally everyone drove in the middle of the road, reluctant to turn off into the rutted part until the last possible moment. The result was a succession of near misses. Water buffaloes pulling carts with their drivers half asleep on the loads, lumbered along in the centre, and only crossed over to the soft edges as the horn blared and brakes screeched within spitting distance to wake the driver up. He, by twisting the tails of his beasts and flaying their scarred rumps, managed to, with shouts and yells, urge them ever so slowly over to let us pass.

'What with the dust and this sort of charade, my hair is rapidly turning white,' lamented Ronnie. 'Ram Singh will you *please* drive more smoothly; every time we pass something the dogs fall off their seats in the back.'

'*Accha, Accha*, Miss-sahib,' Ram Singh grunted as he honked away to absolutely no avail.

'Gosh, what a journey. I'm so *hungry!*' I had to laugh.

It went on; the road by now was crowded beyond belief. Dilapidated buses with wooden sides suddenly seemed determined to overtake one another. Their drivers screamed vituperations as they raced side by side. Jolting tongas with their passengers sitting sideways and crammed in, were forced onto the verges where their drooping ponies were whipped into a reluctant trot. As we came to the bazaar of Sialkot, young men wobbling along on clapped-out bicycles presented another hazard. Half-clad children with fat tummies played in the road, and women in purdah, wearing the *burkha* covering them like a tent from head to dusty foot with only a narrow grid slit for their eyes, slipped like black ghosts through the crowds.

After passing through the hectic, noisy bazaar of open shops and cooking smells, we came into the quiet of a wide empty *maidan* parade ground by the glaringly white bleached Cavalry Lines where down the centuries famous British regiments had stuck out the hot weathers or died in the process. Now that there was little traffic Ram Singh drove on slowly and sedately through the cantonment, past government buildings and private bungalows each well spaced out in their own garden groves of trees, low hedges and colourful flowering beds. The Kashmir winter Residency was similar to one of these old houses built to withstand the heat. It was not a particularly pretentious building, but one equivalent to others inhabited by the more senior officials and Army officers.

Off a short drive the brake came to rest beside a white house built a hundred or so years ago. On three sides windows opened onto deep verandahs looking out to the garden in a series of pillared arches. Chick screens, which could be rolled up or down like blinds as the sun moved round, hung from the arches. These screens, known as *kuss-kuss tatties*, were doused with water in the hot weather to keep the interior cool. When sluiced they gave out the fragrant scent of their roots. From outside the Residency could have been taken for a mosque with its central pointed roof. Inside it was dark and cool and rather eerie. The enormously high ceilings downstairs were plastered over replacing the hanging sails of before. Now electric overhead fans hung from long poles in place of the original cloth *punkahs* pulled to and fro day and night with a rope by a succession of *punkah-wallahs*. The house, on entering it for the first time, did not strike me as having the friendly atmosphere of the Srinagar Residency. This house was more like a tomb...

A shiver of unease passed through me as I entered its dark chill from the sunny warmth of outside where the temperature was akin to a perfect English summer's day. December, January, February, March - four winter months into the new year of 1940. What would they bring?

84

11
The Cantonment

Sheila and Dem were out by the time we arrived at the winter Residency, and it was Ayah with her dimpled smile who received us in the doorway. She had had an uneventful journey with the main convoy and had settled-in the night before. The amazing part about moving house in India - and one was always moving - was how the servants, not much ahead of their employers, invariably had everything organized to receive them including a three course meal.

My high-ceilinged room was barely furnished, with on the concrete floor a thin *durrie* cotton carpet made in the local jail. Ayah had made up the bed, unpacked and put away the contents of my trunk. The only thing missing was my overnight suitcase together with our lorry, the dogs' sweeper and all their accoutrements.

'Did you have a good journey, Ayah?' I asked in greeting.

'*Ji-han, hazoor,*' her little black eyes sparkled. 'Ayah like travel.'

'We didn't. Roy was sick and our lorry never turned up.'

'No bedding roll in Dak bungalow?' Ayah tut-tutted. 'Lorry break down.'

'Who told you? What happened?'

'No one tell Ayah. Ayah know,' she declared in her usual scathing manner while taking in my dishevelled appearance and calling for the *bhisti*, who thin legged in his *dhoti* came staggering into the bathroom with his kerosene-oil tins of boiling water heated over a wood fire in the compound in readiness.

This Residency had no plumbing at all and relied on one stand-pipe in the compound. Ayah added cold water from the earthenware jars standing in the *ghussel khana* until she judged the temperature to be just right. Each of the three downstairs bedrooms in the house were *en suite* with dressing-room and bathroom. *En suite* in fact by no means came up to what the term suggests. Though the dressing-room was big enough to be another bedroom, the bathroom was a small windowless box-like building with a badly fitting outside door into the compound for the sweeper to empty the 'thunder-box' commode. The floor was bare concrete with an enclosure for the zinc hip bath. The floor sloped away to a hole in the wall through which the soapy water ran out when the tub was tipped up, and it was just as well to have a good look round before getting into or out of the tub.

Though as most memsahibs did, Sheila saw that the exit hole was bunged up by chicken wire, often this got dislodged. In any case snakes seemed to be able to worm their way in through the finest of wire. I never had an encounter with a snake in a *ghussel khana* but many were the tales of those that had, and in my bathroom that winter the sweeper killed one of the deadly little black kraits of lethal bite. I used to marvel at the tact of the sweeper who never barged in or even knocked on the outside door when one was in situ, so to speak. Some instinct seemed to tell him when it was vacant. It could not have been a pleasant task emptying the contents of the four *ghussel khanas* into the barrel positioned at the back of the compound. The barrel was collected after dark by a man in a bullock cart, and the buckets were returned by the sweeper clean and smelling hygienically of lysol. The job though had its compensations in that the sweeper was a purveyor of information to the other servants. He was said to know more about the state of one's health than we did. Dysentery and infestations were easy to diagnose, and it was common knowledge that the sweeper knew that the memsahib was pregnant probably before she had fully grasped the fact for herself.

By the time I had bathed and changed, our lorry arrived hissing steam from under its battered radiator and came to rest with our pots and pans, bedrolls and food. Ayah was quite right. They had broken down even before reaching the bottom of the Pass. The bearer and sweeper jumped down from beside the driver to anxiously enquire about the Miss-sahibs and how they had fared without bedding and how the puppies had been fed. We were able to assure that, despite missing them, we had managed. The Kashmiri sweeper went straight into Ronnie's dressing-room where the puppies were installed, and after unpacking their clobber got down to making a pen for them on the verandah so that they could be brought out by day. Sheila and Dem arrived back from having watched a polo match, to hear of our adventures. Sheila then took me round the house.

Though the Sialkot Residency was called a 'bungalow' it had in fact a pent-house second storey on one side of the building with square turret on the other to balance the effect. The pent-house was reached by steep outside steps leading to a suite which Dem and Sheila occupied in seclusion from the rest of the house. Coming down again we progressed into the kitchen, separate and some little distance from the house in the compound area bounded by a low white wall, and found de Souza already settled in. This old kitchen was archaic compared to the large white-tiled integral one in Srinagar. It was a smallish whitewashed room standing on its own, part-blackened by smoke with one naked bulb overhead permanently on in a room made dark by windows covered in heavy gauze to keep flies, mosquitoes and insects out. The gauze door crashed shut on its hinges behind us as we came in to find the space full of passers-by sitting on the mud baked floor. They jumped to their feet salaaming as we entered and then politely went outside in a group till we left. They were friends, or friends of friends, of the servants come in to exchange news since the last winter. Among them came the invaluable *matis* and extra hands to help with the unpacking.

I wondered how de Souza managed to continue to produce superb four course meals on the baked clay stove with its charcoal ovens. *Degchis* bubbled

Front of the Old Kashmir Residency, Sialkot

87

away on the stove. These handleless gleaming saucepans with their flat lids were cleaned by scouring with ashes and sand, and then dried with *jharans*, thick cotton cloths, a dozen of which were used daily in the kitchen for every purpose. No memsahib who was keen on hygiene stinted the number of these invaluable cloths. When dirty they were thrown in a corner for the *dhobi* to collect and wash.

'What are you cooking?' Sheila asked.

'Pastry for apply-pie, Memsahib,' de Souza informed as he heaped red pieces of live charcoal on a flat lid to make an extra oven. He looked as tidy as always in his tight white suit covered with a large apron.

'*Shabash*, it smells good,' praised Sheila. She knew well the difficulties he had in this hot primitive kitchen with a constant battle with flies that got through the swing door, and also with cockroaches, two inch long brown horrors which scuttled along the floor and came out in their hundreds at night despite the powder put to kill them.

'I've given up trying to get him to stop cooking the pastry separately,' Sheila remarked as we wandered through the garden. 'I can't deny that his pastry is excellent even though it is inclined to slide off the pie like a board!'

The garden with its many shady tropical trees had been redesigned by Sheila. There were low hedges in the front dividing patches of lawn with borders of salvias, canna lilies and poinsettias. In view of the front of this house on a plinth, and as a focal point backed by a hedge with herbaceous border on either side, stood a graceful copy of a Grecian urn with sundial atop. Quite different from the Srinagar Residency garden, this one had parched grass and sandy drive, and was set in a cantonment road from where other houses could be seen. Yet it had a tropical beauty of its own, a place to dream away lazy days reading and writing and thinking of other Miss-sahibs in Victorian dresses doing the same.

❦   ❦   ❦   ❦

But there was little time to sit in the old garden and dream. Straight away I was caught up in a whirl of parties and inundated with invitations. Although we still entertained it was mainly to friends the Frasers already knew, and there was no Book for people to sign. That was left to the Commandant of the cantonment who was the senior man there.

In Kashmir the unmarried officers came up on leave for shortish periods and no sooner had they arrived in Srinagar than they disappeared into the surrounding mountains to shoot and fish. This was the famed *shikar*, that admired Hindi word for 'hunting' which conjured up the excitement to be found in mountain or jungle far from habitation with the challenge, the danger, the achievement. Most of the men I met were far keener on *shikar* than wasting their time after other 'birds'.

There were great platonic friendships made amongst men without a whiff of scandal. Anything like that would be pounced on by the CO briefed by the all-knowing Adjutant almost before it happened. The perpetrator would be cashiered. If they wanted a woman they knew where to go, but even that was considered a bit feeble. They were mostly romantics who were prepared to wait for the perfect wife to come along, one who was good-looking enough to be the envy of the Mess, one who could keep up with them in excursions into the jungles for Christmas camps, go on treks into the mountains, bear healthy children and follow them to the ends of the earth - and all within the limits of their fairly meagre pay, a tall order! The only 'scandals' I came across in Sialkot were between officers and married women, some in the same regiment to cause heartbreak and havoc. At that time divorce was not permitted unless under exceptional or tragic circumstances such as certifiable insanity.

That winter in Sialkot were stationed several elements of the Frontier Force, including the 10/12th Frontier Force Regiment, the 2nd Royal Lancers (Gardner's Horse, about to say goodbye to their chargers in a grand parade), the 3rd Carabiniers, the PAVOs (the ebullient polo playing Carr-White I seem to remember), and many more, beside all the rest of Gunners, Sappers, Signals, REME, Staff Officers and so on whom I hardly cottoned on to in my first introduction to a large army station.

I found that there were no unmarried girls whatsoever in Sialkot to make friends with, but instead an absolute posse of subalterns, eligible Captains, Majors and even bachelor Lieutenant-Colonels had I come out with the 'Fishing Fleet' to hook a husband! I rather prided myself that I had *not*. On the death of my beloved American grandmother who had brought me up, I had started out to circle the world, first stops in Africa successfully accomplished, and then India for a year or so - where it looked as if I had been caught by the war - before going on to the Far East of Hong Kong, China and Japan with friends and relations to visit all the way.

The wives of the more senior officers, with whom I made many friends, and who one and all were determined to get me married off, spent much time playing bridge - as Sheila did - with mahjong sessions in the mornings, all of which I managed to avoid on the excuse (there was little work for Dem) of my daily *munshi* lessons with Patsy, who together with a recovered Michael lived near. There were Ladies dinners in the various Messes to which I was invited, Club dances, tennis at the Club or on the Residency's one red court. A great deal of time seemed to be spent watching Dem playing cricket on the mat-covered pitch, and of course there was polo.

Nearly all officers played polo whether Cavalry or not. Their regard for their horses was rated higher than anything else. It was said when they married, their love for their wives came second to their mounts! Too, many of these bronzed fit young men skied well. For equipment they had long, heavy, hickory skis with leather straps binding their boots. These were bought together with their polo sticks and tennis rackets at 'Uberoi's' of Sialkot known far and wide in India. At week-ends several officers together would drive in an old 'banger' up the snow-bound passes to Gulmarg way above Srinagar for the winter sport. When up there at over 8,000 feet, they had to climb every inch of the way to the tops of the runs on fur skins attached to their skis.

Every year the Army officer in India was entitled to two months 'privileged' leave to give him a break from working in the hot weather, when the plains became an inferno till the monsoon broke, when things were not all that much better. The dampness was almost as enervating as the heat. Leather became coated with green mildew overnight which caused endless extra work to other ranks in the cleaning of boots and equipment. (I often felt the ORs were better off than the officers in that they were allowed to marry when younger and most of them in Sialkot had wives and children with them in good quarters where they luxuriated in having servants.) Often officers spent their privileged leave in even greater discomfort by booking a forest block to shoot game in the Central Provinces, said to be the hottest province of all. In addition to this leave officers were allowed three casual leaves a year, such as Stuart had taken in the autumn. This leave of up to ten days did not count against annual leave.

Then once every three years he was granted home leave of eight months to include the journey by train and P & O liner. Flying took three days. The nights were spent at airport hotels, and was only just beginning to be used when the war started, and all home leave was cancelled. This long leave was the time when many officers took the opportunity to get married, probably to a girl met at home on their previous leave and written to regularly since. According to which Corps or regiment he was in (they varied) an officer was not expected to get married before the age of thirty. Of course many did, but it was tough on their families unless they had private means, and it could adversely affect their promotion: 'tied by the apron strings instead of volunteering for the Frontier' etc. Towards the end of 1939 it was still considered by the stalwarts that to succumb to marriage before thirty was rather weak-kneed and 'letting the Regiment down'.

In this environment Miss-sahibs could not fail to have many proposals. Even Ronnie in her middle-aged spinsterhood had her followers, though that winter she was on the whole much too busy with the puppies to take notice of men. Happily she hummed about her work, her cigarette bouncing jauntily on her lips as she tended, fussed over and fed them.

But though fulfilled with the dogs, all was not happy with Ronnie. Underneath the mannish exterior I had found a sensitive nature which needed tactful handling, for Ronnie easily took offence. Any aside or even observation could be taken as a personal slight, and sparks sometimes flew between her and Dem. As his idea of a joke was a schoolboy type of humour, sometimes made out of curiosity to see what the reaction would be, Ronnie was often hurt. Dem could not understand why she did not take it as the bit of fun it was meant to be, and was unable to resist the temptation to tease despite Sheila at times telling him in no uncertain terms to 'lay off'. It got to such a pitch that Sheila and I tried to see that they were never left alone together for any length of time when Dem would quickly get bored with her endless going on about the puppies. She talked of nothing else but their progress, their weight, their de-worming results, and their different personalities and characteristics.

꽃   꽃   꽃   꽃

As Christmas approached there were so many invitations for us in the Residency that, to avoid any accusation of discrimination, we would accept several cocktail parties on the same evening, stay at each for short periods before making our excuses to go on to a dinner party given by the Station Commander or one of the Commanding Officers.

I found myself particularly taken up by the Carabiniers who were considered by other regiments to 'think rather a lot of themselves.' To me they were the most amusing fun fellows, all very close-knit in their doings, and I was flattered when I found myself drawn into their exclusive circle. They had a 'chummery' of subalterns who lived in a bungalow they named the 'Blue Church'. It became the setting for hilarious parties after reckless games of polo, and of course I fell in love with one of them, James Allason who became an MP. I called him 'Maurice' because he reminded me of my brother who at that time was piloting a Lancaster Bomber with a load of bombs destined for Germany. At one point, when limping home, the aircraft getting lower and lower, he handling it brilliantly, it gave up and came down in the Channel. For a few terrible struggling moments, Maurice could not open the cockpit. Just in time he did, and was in the end picked up, still alive, from the freezing sea. So James, charming, good-looking, tall and dark-haired, became a special friend, as did Tony Johnson of the PAVOs, especially liked for his humour and magnificent height of six-foot seven. I called him 'Little John'.

The Blue Church boys drank a lot and at the Club one of them - not James who had learnt to 'hold his drink'- fell over backwards while we were dancing and brought me down on top of him to lie in a heap on the ballroom floor. Mercifully Dem was not there that evening for he would have made a scene and frog-marched the young man off and probably informed his CO about the undignified incident as well, and demand that he was severely reprimanded. As for me I was mortified in the extreme. It was the most blush-making thing that had ever happened to me, and in front of all those COs and their wives who would no doubt think I had led the subaltern on. The shame of it lived with me until something far more serious happened to banish the incident from my mind.

But though I never danced with that particular man again, I still went to the Blue Church chummery because of James, who appeared to be as fond of me as I was of him, and because of 'Little John' who really was an absolute darling and told me he 'carried the torch' for me - whatever that meant. These mostly well-heeled cavalry men whose 'steeds' were now tanks, also gambled in their Blue Church. I don't know, but I imagine this was 'against orders'. They played hard at games with their men, walked hard on manoeuvres, climbed hard on skiing or mountaineering expeditions, worked hard in their offices and threw money away on the green baize. But the toughest time of all was playing polo on the dry hard ground where bones got broken, heads were bashed, limbs bruised. During that winter in Sialkot there was a death on the field; even that appeared to be accepted as part of the price for the skill and thrill of chasing a bamboo ball on a pony.

The game could be equally dangerous to the spectators from the bazaar who, from the *babus* in the offices and the shopkeepers, to the servants in the houses, came out in their numbers to line the ground and cheer the sahibs on. With only a white line to show the boundary, they pressed forwards onto the field the better to see, the crowd scattering with yells of laughter as sweating flanks and flaying hooves rode into them.

Then the ball was thrown in, play started off again in a mêlée of legs, until with a spurt of dust and rattle of hoofs on the iron ground, in no time all that could be seen was the arc of a swinging stick through billows of white dust. As the tournament progressed the games became tougher and tougher, until the Final arrived in a deadly battle, each side prepared to die to win the prized silver Cup on the stand behind which the Resident's lady sat ready to hand to the sweating but beaming captain of the victorious team.

Did it prepare them for war - harden them? I suppose so. It was not long before they were all up to their necks in the real thing.

12
Survival

Sialkot was situated on an excessively flat plain with not a hill nor an incline in sight. It was the perfect place for bicycling. Everyone, rich or poor, bicycled. Not wishing to be dependent on the Residency cars to take me to my various engagements, I asked Dost Mohammed to hire a lady's steed from the bazaar. I should mention here that there was no need to *buy* anything in India. If the item was not to be found in the bazaar, word got round and a selection soon appeared to hire, whether it was a bicycle, equipment of any sort, or the furniture necessary to add to the quartermaster's bare essentials.

I loved to bicycle. The weather was perfect and it gave me the freedom to peddle off at will to friends' bungalows or to visit the boys in the Blue Church. But the sun could be hot from midday onwards. Though few knew the real danger of pollution or skin cancer in those days when not so long before sun bathing in Europe had become a craze, the danger of too much sun had been known by the military from when they wore pads for protection down the spine. I had noticed that even in winter many people in Sialkot wore *topis*, and I had dug out of my tin-lined trunk the sun helmet I had had in Kenya where the doctor with whom I was staying told me that 'too much sun raddled the brain'. I was innocently bicycling off down the Residency drive when there was a bellow from the tennis court where a foursome was in progress:

'Take that ghastly thing off at once,' Dem shouted while the rest gaped.

'Why...what on earth...well, I mean, what's wrong with it?' I braked and skidded to a standstill in the red dust.

'There's nothing WRONG with it as such; you can't wear it, that's all.'

I was baffled. The statement seemed to me far from logical. Sheila was sitting nearby working on her tapestry and watching the tennis, so I wheeled my bicycle up to her and demanded an explanation.

She gave me a half smile. 'It's just that we don't wear round white ones like those,' she said lamely. 'They're known as missionary *topis*, and, well....in our circles it's not done. We wear khaki ones, and of a different shape. Silly really.'

I agreed. I thought it excessively silly, but out of deference to their feelings, I gave the offending headgear to de Mello who wore it on his bald head. In place, I took to wearing my double-felted *terai*, also bought in Kenya, which was accepted at the Residency as 'very becoming'. The white *topi* had been *de rigeur* in the highlands of Kenya, but not in society in India. Even Ronnie would not wear a white *topi*, so she said. But then Ronnie's parentage was fairly upper-class. To me this British class system on which people laid much emphasis in India, was not only incomprehensible but stupid. So I tackled James on the subject. If anyone was high society the Carabiniers were. He roared with laughter and dared me to go on wearing my white topi. I told him it now reposed on de Mello's bald head at which he fell about laughing the more.

'I really don't see what's so funny,' I said crossly.

'You're funny. You're an innocent unaware of the rituals. You bring a breath of fresh air to the place. You're not a bit like an English deb.'

'I'm not one. I was offered a season in London and I turned it down; said I'd prefer to travel round the world. I'm half Irish and I was brought up by an American grandmother in France.'

'Ah, that accounts for it. Humn. Stay that way....'

'What way?'

'Far-seeing and broad minded,' James said and he squeezed my hand. I was enormously flattered.

⚘   ⚘   ⚘   ⚘

On Christmas day, Dem, Sheila, Ronnie and I went to the Garrison Church packed with ultra smart troops and officers in tropical uniforms with shining Sam Browne belts. Afterwards the Carabiniers gave a drink party in their Mess for practically the whole Cantonment. I conversed with the Blue Church boys Leyland, Sandford and Pain by shouting to one another above the sound of the regimental band on the sun-drenched lawn, a band which played, full blast, extracts from the 'Light Cavalry Overture' and 'The Maid of the Mountains.'

We returned for a lunch party at the decorated Residency which we had made to look festive on the day before. The head *mali* had produced a pine tree on which to hang our gifts. The *sanghur* heads on the walls in the hall together with the pillars had been made colourful with trails of the cerise bougainvillaea which romped over the walls outside. Scarlet poinsettias from the garden gave the house the right colour for a Christmassy look. Sheila showed me the trick of burning the stems first with lighted matches to stop the sap from running which had the effect of preserving the branches for weeks.

After Christmas came a Fancy Dress Ball with the men hard to recognize dressed up in Arab costume or as Egyptian potentates with red fezes, after which came the highlight of the New Year. This was Sialkot Week when the 'cold' weather was at its best and there was something on every day from Paper Chases on bicycles to Treasure and Scavenging Hunts for impossible items such as an English Bobby's helmet or a baby's feeding bottle. Who'd last had a baby? And everyone rushed off to inundate the young wife in that particular bungalow.

It was all great fun but the most amusing event was invariably the *pagal*

Joan Battye, Sheila Fraser and author on Residency steps, Srinagar

(mad) gymkhana. This bullock-cart race with a lady at the helm, always caused great mirth. I must admit that I had not laughed so much since my schoolgirl prank days. The idea was to manoeuvre the two-span cumbrous animals along a race course, with the span drawing a running two-wheeled vehicle called a *ringi* driven by a woman with a man at her side to assist her. Tony, 'Little John', was my partner. Our span insisted on going round and round in a circle instead of towards the finishing post no distance away. Everyone watching was in hysterics as Tony's flaying arms took over the reins which only made matters worse. It really was hugely funny. No-one won as all the beasts wandered off their own ways into the countryside from where we had to be rescued by the owners. But we were voted the best entertainment and given a consolation prize.

By contrast this farce was followed by the Trick Rides, as good as a circus turn with so many expert riders in the Station who had passed out from the exacting Saugor Equestrian School. There were displays of bareback riding with men and officers standing aloft, and of horses dancing in time to the music. Others were made to lie down until told to scramble to their feet again. I felt this was a bit unfair. I was sure they did not in the least want to lie down though James told me the training had saved many a charger's life on the Frontier when in a defile they had kept their horses quiet until the danger passed by sitting at their heads, and stroking their nozzles. Even so these beautifully groomed beasts looked to me ungainly and uncomfortable with their big bellies heaving in the dust.

Soon after the Week, and still in January, came a big event in Ronnie's life when Glory and her puppies were due to go to the Dog Show in Lahore further down the Grand Trunk Road from Sialkot. The puppies were by now weaned and in excellent health. Even Pickles looked plump. There was no excuse for Ronnie to hang on to them any longer, and the very reason for their existence had become urgent. Yes, money was needed to bring the boys out at the end of the summer term. Sheila had prevailed, and it did seem a sensible decision, especially as Eric Tyndale-Biscoe, the son of the old Canon, who had been persuaded to divert and become his father's deputy when on his way to farm in New Zealand, was now starting a school in Kashmir for British Officers' sons who had been caught by the war.

Sheila and I decided to go to the Dog Show with Ronnie. We left her there while we strolled round the Shalimar Gardens, so different from the setting of the gardens in lake and mountains. This Moghul garden lay flat with a wall round its forty acres. Nevertheless it was beautiful in its lay-out of broad walks between beds of shrubs, pomegranate trees, splashing waterways and fountains land-scaped before the graceful white marbled tomb of the famous Ranjit Singh.

96

With a little time in hand before we were due to pick up Ronnie, we went to see Kim's Gun upon which the child sat in the Kipling novel. In the middle of fast moving traffic by the Museum, (set up by Lockwood Kipling, Rudyard's father) there it still stood for tourists to admire. Cast in 1760 it was used at the battle of Panipat and the siege of Multan, and it was believed that whoever held the gun was the master of the Punjab.

꙳   ꙳   ꙳   ꙳

On the way home Ronnie proudly told us of the high offer for four of the puppies she had had from the Nawab of Dir who would be in touch with Dem over the transaction. Since the advent of the puppies Ronnie had been a different person, busy all day and half the night with them and totally fulfilled. She adored the puppies on whom she lavished her mother-love, their needs supplying her need to be needed. Ronnie told Dem about the Nawab's offer, and Sheila suggested that of the remaining puppies, Medlar, of beige colouring, should be given to Stuart - who had wanted to have one - as a present. (As a reward for her work, Ronnie had already chosen Simon for herself, the most blonde puppy of the litter.) 'Good idea,' Dem said with regard to Stuart. 'The fuss that has gone on over the lot. I shall be glad to see the last of them.'

As well as getting to know Ronnie since coming to India, I had also got to know Dem. He was an extremely capable administrative officer of some thirty years standing, painstaking and serious over his work. But in private he could behave like a schoolboy. He loved to play the buffoon when we four were 'en famille', so to speak. Then he would tease us, blue eyes goggling, grey moustache twitching. He adored his talented Sheila - and she had virtually become a semi-invalid, on occasions staying in her room in her dressing-gown for several days at a time, when Ronnie and I would stand in as hostesses. But then we too had been ill: I once with the usual Indian 'tummy' so severe that I had feared it was dysentery, and Ronnie, laid up with a re-occurrence of sand-fly fever she had had on a previous visit to India. To cap it all 'Little John' was taken to hospital with heart trouble. I visited him there - he looked so uncomfortable in the far too short cot, that my heart quite went out to him.

During this period, when recovering from my indisposition in my lofty room, I felt more than ever that the Sialkot Residency was haunted by its past. I had had no experience of the supernatural before, neither did I have 'the sight' as Sheila had from her mother in Scotland. I did not broach the subject, but when feeling low in my room at night it seemed to me the house was full of ghosts from the days of the mutiny of 1857. Sheila had told me how rebellious sepoys had fought in Sialkot setting fire to bungalows, and had at one point chased a wife and her children into this house and murdered them, and that their bodies had been buried in the garden, she would not say where. But I knew: under the peepul

97

tree. Then too there had been a cholera epidemic in the Cantonment when many had died, some again in this house. Was there a vendetta against us European women in the Residency? Or was I just imagining it because I was feeling rotten?

Things came to a head when Dem found himself, changed into his dinner-jacket, sitting alone at the head of an empty table with only the stags' heads on the high walls for company. Waiting on him with de Mello were two *khitmagars*. More worried about his wife's health than he let on, and hating to be on his own, Dem poured out his spleen on the servants.

'*Idder ao amak ka baccha. Jaldi, jaldi kara kambakht*, come here quickly you numbskull,' he shouted to one waiter.

'*Ek dam, huzoor. Ji-han, sahib*,' the man jumped to it, his face staying impassive under the verbal onslaught, 'at once, sahib.'

'Better keep your wits about you,' I heard de Mello counselling in the hall as the *khitmagars* brought the food over from the kitchen, 'the Colonel-sahib is in a temper tonight!'

'The Colonel-sahib's bark is worse than his bite,' the waiters grinned at one another, their loyalty to him apparently unimpaired. In fact it was how *they* treated their wives. A man in India was a man and the undoubted master of his household who obeyed his every wish. If the burra-sahib did not show his temper from time to time he would be a lesser man for that!

But as the days went by even the pleasure of knowing she could keep Simon did not make up for Ronnie the thought of losing the others. After the morning when the Nawab of Dir sent his henchmen down to collect the four puppies, she mooched round the house on tiptoe as if there had been a death, her cigarette barely held on downcast lower lip.

'Cheer up Ronnie,' I tried to encourage, 'you've still got four dogs in the house.'

'I'm so afraid the little darlings won't be properly looked after by those Indians,' she wrinkled up her forehead.

'Nonsense. They are such valuable dogs they're bound to give them the very best of attention. They wouldn't buy them just to neglect them...'

'Still...it's not the same...'

At dinner that night, with Sheila once again in bed in her pent-house upstairs - the local doctor was undecided as to the cause: it could be gall-bladder trouble, or it could be a grumbling appendix - and there were only three of us round the table, Dem was extremely tactless to say the least.

'Thank God those bloody puppies have gone,' he aired in relief as he tackled the soup, 'now perhaps the fuss will die down and we'll have some peace - anyway we got a good price for them.'

Ronnie burst into tears and rushed from the table. Dem turned to look at me with bushy eye-brows raised.

'What on earth's got into *her*?' he said.

98

¥   ¥   ¥   ¥

Few people escaped long in India without becoming ill, but Dem was one of the lucky ones. Tough and wiry and extremely fit as he was, he found it difficult to sympathize with the everyday ailments of life that attacked lesser mortals, particularly, it seemed to me, us women at the Sialkot Residency. We, he implied, succumbed out of weak-mindedness If we tried harder surely we could overcome it?

We certainly could not have been more hygienically looked after with Sheila at the helm. De Souza kept his kitchen spotlessly clean, and the servants were periodically tested to see there were no carriers. Anything eaten raw from fruit to lettuce and tomatoes was washed carefully in a strong solution of 'pinky-pani', red permanganate of potash crystals dissolved in water. Despite all precautions most people had a bout of dysentery, and in the plains everyone had malaria.

These latter attacks - I had one go - were shattering and distinct with aching limbs, a bad head, burning hot one minute and shivering cold the next. One's temperature rose to a peak at the same time daily and then plummeted to leave one weak and shaky. The bitter pink quinine pills which made the head and ears buzz, cured quickly, but reinfection was common. There was supposed to be no malaria in the winter when the mosquitoes could not survive the cold. Mosquito nets were put away and no prophylactic pills were issued; even so people went down with malaria. 'In the blood' they said, 'the cold weather brings it out'. Sand-fly fever was not considered so serious, but was deemed to be a depressing illness which rest would cure. Amoebic dysentery - an extremely debilitating illness - was treated with a course of emertine injections said to affect the heart, so that the patient was advised to take no exercise for three weeks. As for Sheila, the Commandant of the Military Hospital in Sialkot, Colonel Bridges, and our Residency Surgeon, George Ledgard, put their heads together and came to the conclusion that Sheila's trouble was more likely to be gall-stones than inflamed appendicitis, and that she should be operated on on our return to Kashmir.

We three women had all recovered somewhat, though I was in a state of exhaustion from the sheer pace of Sialkot Week during which I prided myself I had not missed a single 'do', when one morning I awoke with a severe headache. For two days I fought it knowing full well the outburst it would precipitate from Dem. The impossibility of becoming ill again in this household kept me staggering on through a dinner party at the Residency. I watched myself dispassionately at my most vivacious in leading the conversation, noting the men's admiring glances. Never had I been so popular, never so good at stimulating the conversation and making the party 'go'. As if through a shimmering hazy curtain I saw myself flushed and laughing and knew that I was delirious.

Later, I crept between the cool white sheets of my bed, my head burning and throbbing with pain, to lie awake listening to the pounding of my heart for the rest of that long, long night when the ghosts of the haunted Residency came to taunt. Above me, instead of the flat ceiling, there billowed the 'sails' of old through which I could see the indentation of snakes as they wormed themselves across the roof space, and could hear the rustling of civet cats about their business. Owls screeched in the garden echoing the shrieks of the women and children butchered in my room in the Mutiny. Jackals that roamed in packs round the town at night, just as they had those seventy years ago, howled eerily near to the verandahs to terrify. By first light, my eyes bright with sleeplessness and fever, I found that when Ayah came in with my *chota hazri*, I could not lift my head off the pillow to sip the tea she brought.

George Ledgard was summoned. He took my temperature, looked at the thermometer once and then again in disbelief. He marched from the room without saying anything. An army ambulance arrived at the door of the old bungalow. Strong khaki-clad orderlies laid me gently onto a stretcher. Outside the dazzling glare pierced my eyes in a blinding agony; then I was in the hot shade of the ambulance.

❦   ❦   ❦   ❦

At the beginning of my illness I remember little but how I could not sleep until they gave me morphia. After that blessed interlude scenes flickered before me like quick snapshots between feverish nightmares. Doctors in white coats bent over me. One had cool probing hands. Another, a nurse, held a feeding cup to my lips, and tipped the spout so that I could sip from it. Her hands were brown with thumbs and fingers that curved back. They placed icy damp bags packed round my body, and a cool flannel on my brow to bring a temporary relief from the furnace. The tossing days and nights merged and still I could not sweat and always I was in agony from the aching, bursting, head.

I dreamed of being a child again in Menton and of Marie lulling me to sleep:

'Fais do do, mon petit frère,
Fais do do, t'auras du lolo.'

I woke but kept my eyes shut to stay with my lovely dream of childhood, to swim in the joy of it again and again repeating the words of the lullaby while the dream was still vivid in my memory.

The call to prayer became another nightmare, a repeated dreaded one which roused me from mixed-up sleep to terrify me. Very early it started as dawn began to break. It came from a balcony atop a high minaret close to the hospital. The banshee-like voice of the Muezzin flowed and receded in a penetrating la-la-la wail that struck an inexplicable terror into my heart. I was being tortured in a fiery hell. I was dying and I would go to hell where the banshee voices were waiting to revile me.

I blocked my ears with my fingers in an endeavour to keep out the terrifying voice of the Muezzin, but nothing would obliterate the penetrating sound so close to where I lay. Reprieve when the bantam cocks began to crow, a short lived cheerful moment to be replaced all too soon by the maddening brain fever bird raucously repeating and repeating all through the blinding day, endlessly telling me - as if I did not already know it - 'brain-fever, brain-fever, brain-fever'.

Tap-tap, tap-tap, tap-tap went the nurse's high heels on the bare sanitary floor of my cell. I was driven to screaming pitch by the sound: tap-tap, tap-tap, tap-tap... '

'Ayah, take off your shoes,' I shouted at her unable to bear it any longer. But the brain-fever bird and the tap-tapping went on and on.

My shoulder length golden hair was hot around my neck. They cut it off in chunks, yet nothing could ease my pain. I was parched with thirst but my throat was so sore that I could barely swallow the sips of cooling drinks they brought in the feeding cup. Neither could I breathe. I could hear my breath wheezing out in strangled gasps through my open mouth; in-out, in-out, in-out. I then became conscious of the doctor with the cool hands bending over me. 'I'm going to give you an injection, Miss Hart,' he said. Miss Hart? Was that me lying here? It did not feel like me... I felt the deep jab go into my thigh muscles. The injection forced my eyes open and made me cry out in pain. Looking down where my nightgown had been lifted I saw that my naked skin was covered in a red rash.

When next I opened my eyes it was to see a Padre in khaki uniform with black dicky and white collar sitting in a chair drawn-up beside my bed.

'We prayed for you at the Parade Service this morning,' he said, seeing I was awake.

Then a dark despair overwhelmed me. He was going to give me the Last Rites! I was dying! I thought of England, England where I had been born but which had never been my home. I longed for England with an extraordinary intensity, not the Menton of my childhood. Why England where I had been ill treated and neglected in a horrible Home before my grandmother had come to the rescue and taken me away to live with her in the sunshine - where lemons grew. Menton was my real home. My mother was buried in Shanghai. She too knew she was dying. What were her thoughts as she lay the world away from her handsome little dark-haired Maurice, and me so fair? Four years old, and two years old. Maurice could remember her singing: I had no recollection of her soft loveliness. She had died but I did not want to die, not here, not in this foreign land

101

of India to be buried on the very day of my last breath deep down in the sandy blackness of what the troops called the 'Padre's godown', far far away from the cool comfort of an English graveyard with its damp smell of rotting leaves. Here they would have to take a pickaxe to get through the ground to bury me! No I did not want to die in a foreign land as my mother had when she was only a few years older than I was now, but at least had known married love and children. In Shanghai they had cremated her. In India they buried... and so quickly. Hot tears splashed down my cheeks.

'I am too young. I am not ready to die!' I clutched at the startled Padre's hand.

The heat burst from me in a pouring sweat of rivulets soaking the bed under my body.

They smiled and sponged me down. They held me sitting while they put on a fresh nightgown. Then, lying me down, they left me to sleep, and sleep... and sleep...

13
Convalescence

All was extraordinarily quiet when I awoke to an unaccustomed hush. For a moment I could not explain it, then I realized the relentless drumming in my head had ceased. I lay still and looked about me with interest. I was on my own in a small white room, lying flat on my back in bed with no pillow. The French window leading onto a verandah was wide open; the flowered curtains waved in a breeze. I became aware that some time must have gone by since I had been carted out from the Residency on a stretcher, for I could sense that the sun was higher and beating down more hotly outside. My eyes wandered to watch a *chipkali* clinging motionless to the wall beside me. I smiled at the remembrance of the geckos that had come out of the thatched hut on Bamburi beach when I was in Kenya before I came to India. It all seemed a long time ago.

A nurse bustled into the room, her high heels tap tapping. She picked up my wrist to feel my pulse. 'You-are-much-better my deeear. Let me get you a pillow,' she smiled. She was a small Anglo-Indian woman with a broad nose and beautiful brown eyes. She was dressed in a starched white overall with a nurse's three-cornered veil tied over dark crinkled short hair.

'What would you like to eet to-dayee?' she asked in rapid sing-song speech after placing one thin pillow under my head.

At the mention of food I was all at once hungry - ravenously hungry. 'More than anything in the world I'd like a kipper!' I said, thinking of the delicious saltiness of it.

'Well, you certainly are better,' she answered with a tinkling laugh, 'there are no such things as kippers in Sialkot, but I'll see what we can do about getting some up from Bombay, shall we?'

'What is your name?' I enquired later after I had had my first solid food since being admitted to hospital.

'Mrs Tapsall,' she replied, 'I am a private nurse. My hubby works in the Families Hospital, Indian Medical Department. Since you are infectious you had to be isolated and the two of us, my hubby and me, were put on to look after you as an urgent case. There is a little kitchen across the passage where I do the cooking for you. That is why you can order anything you like.'

'Do you sleep here? Are you here at nights too?'

'Dear me no! Give me a chance! You have a night nurse. But my hubby is always on call for you. He was over quite a bit at nights at first.' A tall thin man walked in. I looked at his hands and recognized them as the cool capable ones

103

that had attended me and given the injection. He was Doctor Tapsall, darker skinned than his wife but with the same Indian accent.

'Ah, that's more like it, Miss Hart,' he declared briskly after examining me.'

'What is wrong with me doctor? What happened? I... I don't remember much.'

'You have scarlet fever and diphtheria all mixed up, and as if that were not enough, developed jaundice on top. All three in one go! A most unusual case, most interesting,' he looked at me as if I was a fascinating specimen of laboratory flesh. 'Once we were able to diagnose the three diseases - highly infectious in the case of two, a medical team came up from Delhi with the diphtheria serum to study the case. The new injection saved your life. Amazing. Your throat began to clear up within twenty-four hours of having received it, otherwise we would have had to do a tracheotomy, that is inserted a tube in your throat.'

'Horrors', I said with meaning. Diphtheria! I had once seen a film in London of a ward where patients had strangled to death. I was only a twelve year old child at the time and why I had been taken I cannot imagine. It had haunted me for years and now I had had it and survived. 'No more hauntings,' I said out loud.

Dr Tapsall looked at me curiously. 'At present all you have to do is to get strong again,' he expressed while bracing his shoulders as if this was how I could do it. 'Lots of rest, lots of nourishing food. My wife will help you build up your strength,' he ended biffing her on the behind as he left the room.

I felt quite important. If one had to be so horribly ill, one might as well go the whole hog and become something of a phenomenon. But I did not feel so good when I remembered how Mrs Tapsall's steps in her heeled shoes had driven me mad and I had shouted out calling her 'ayah'. That word I knew would be considered an insult by an educated Indian who wore shoes and often a smart hat to church with their dressy European clothes.

'I'm sorry. I believe I shouted at you...' I faltered. I felt the blush rising.

'You talked a lot of nonsense,' Mrs Tapsall chuckled, 'half the time you were babbling away in French which unfortunately I cannot understand!'

❀   ❀   ❀   ❀

I learnt a great deal about the Tapsalls in the weeks to come. They were utterly loyal to their British nationality and called the United Kingdom 'home' though neither of them had ever been there. They were, down the years, the result of liaisons between native women and British Other Ranks, which, whether marriages or not, were still happening in India all the time to produce quite beautiful children, many far better looking that the pure British or pure Indian. As far as I could see the only thing to 'give them away' so to speak (a term I use only because they so passionately wished to be British), were their hands with their moon nails and flexible fingers, the capable kind hands I had noticed holding the feeding cup, the strong little hands of Ayah. More often than not the men were employed in the Railway service, the enormous and complicated network which they ran all over India with the utmost efficiency. Others made first class doctors and superb nurses on whom the British greatly depended. The Tapsalls here had become a well-known team in Sialkot called in by the local hospitals for the difficult, seriously ill and most infectious cases. The Tapsalls told me about their only child, a son who wanted to train to be a doctor but had foregone that to join up on the outbreak of war. They proudly showed me a snapshot of him in uniform embarking for Singapore.

I called her 'Tappy', (what else with her tapping high-heeled steps on the bare floor?) and it was she who drew me back into life. Patiently, brightly she nursed me in my weakness.

'Legs up, legs up Mrs Brown,' she sang as she brought in the bed pan, 'coo-er they're like sticks!' She coaxed me into eating more. In the room across the passage she whipped up raw eggs laced with brandy and flavoured with orange or vanilla. The kippers arrived all the way from Bombay, and boy, were they delicious! Dr Tappy came in often to see me though there was no more for him to do other than to monitor my progress. Colonel Bridges, the mighty Commandant, came in every now and then to see how the 'Senior Service' was getting on.

'Can I have another pillow?' one day I asked Tappy.

'No, not yet.'

'Why not?' I asked plaintively.

'You have to be careful,' she answered as sternly as Tappy could make herself be which was not stern at all.

'You have to be careful,' she repeated. 'Diphtheria affects the heart you know.'

'No, I didn't know.' Whatever the nationality, wherever in the world the patient is, with the invalid so grateful, so totally dependent, there develops that special intimate relationship between nurse and patient. In my case I felt my love for Tappy was too strong ever to be loosened. She was everything to me during that hospital time. I was devoted to her, held no secrets from her, never wanted her to leave me. She knew all about the tragedy of my childhood and how with my father's remarriage I had for some years been placed in a Home where I was neglected, badly treated and permanently scarred. She knew about my grandmother who had eventually rescued me and about Marie, our *bonne-à-tout-faire*, who, dark, swarthy, and moreover with a limp since childhood and a cleft palate, had lulled me to sleep with her village songs from the ancient fortress of her mountain home. She knew about my boy friends and how, after my brush with death, my great wish now was to get married and have children of my own to make up for my lack of family - and quickly. There was urgency in my wish now, while before I had just wanted to see the world and have a good time. Now marriage was imperative before there were any more illnesses to inhibit, before the war hotted up and the men went off to be killed. But who to marry? The Blue Church boys were subalterns, and too young to think of marriage yet awhile.

I had grown to be so dependent on Tappy both physically and mentally that the thought of going out into the world again to pick up the threads of life and find a husband for myself outside the clinical safe walls of the Isolation Ward filled me with alarm. Added to this I dreaded the thought of going back to the old Residency with its ghosts lurking in the lofty rooms, with Sheila often indisposed, with Ronnie often unhappy, with me having let Dem down badly and a pain in the neck I was sure. I had heard how when my illness had been diagnosed they had had to fumigate my room, burn my books and letters and generally disinfect the main rooms of the Residency.

'Can I come and live with you in your bungalow when I am better, Tappy? What will I do without you if I feel faint or come over all peculiar?'

She just laughed at me and sang 'Legs up Mrs Brown' again, and gave me a second pillow. One day she handed me a hand-mirror warning me beforehand to be prepared for a shock. But the warning did not prepare me. And what a shock it was! I did not recognise myself. My hair was chopped short, straight, all perm grown out. Horrified I put a comb through it and found it fell out in handfuls. What was left of it was a dull mouse colour, all the thick gold I was rather proud of gone forever. As for my face: sunken eyes with dark shadows and hollow cheeks in a skin left yellow from jaundice and peeling from the scarlet fever. I looked just like the pictures of the famine children in Calcutta.

'Oh, Tappy,' I wailed, 'how awful I look. No one will want to marry me now.'

'While there's life there's hope,' she chirruped. 'Perhaps it's a good thing. Now someone will love you for yourself and not just for your pretty looks.'

'Some backhanded compliment,' I grunted. But I was pleased to think I had once been pretty.

No one was allowed into my room because of the infection, but at last I could have visitors standing outside. Swallowing my pride I faced the young men from the 'Blue Church' who had sent me fruit and flowers, James among them who reminded me of Maurice who had been awarded the DFC. They came for short periods one at a time so as not to tire me. James, darkly handsome, stood on the verandah by the open French window bearing champagne and peering at me. 'My God, you look awful,' he said chattily. 'What *have* they done to your hair?' They came often bearing pheasants and partridges they had shot in the hills, to whet my appetite. They told tall tales of their skiing exploits in Gulmarg, and made me green with envy. Dem came. He grinned at me from a safe distance and said that I'd given them an awful scare when I was carted off more dead than alive, and that he wanted me back in the office in Srinagar as soon as I was fit enough. I was very pleased and touched about that. Sheila came looking beautiful and bosomy but drawn-faced for all that. Ronnie came with Simon and Medlar on leads. 'Buck up and come back to the Residency. We Miss-sahibs must stick together,' she said jauntily and proceeded to train the two dogs to 'sit' on the verandah. She told me it had been arranged that we were to go into the Cottage on the drive in Srinagar so that there would be more rooms in the Residency for guests with the season coming up. She got quite excited about the prospect. 'Let's get a piano for the sitting-room. It'll be fun; we can entertain our own friends there, and if either of us does have to have a meal in bed, Dem won't notice so much. We're to run the show when Sheila goes in for her operation. They call it an exploratory one now.'

All the while I was getting stronger. Every day Tappy made me sit up and dangle my feet over the side of the bed. It felt funny being upright, and my legs were a travesty of legs without calves, the knees sticking out in boney knobs making my feet look flat and enormous. To my surprise when I put them to the ground I found I could not stand. I had to learn to walk all over again with Tappy supporting my first tentative steps. It felt so peculiar. There I was towering over sturdy little Tappy who until now I had only looked up to. Getting dressed was the next hurdle. My shoulder blades stuck out behind me like sprouting wings; my busts were non existent and my summer dresses, which Sheila had brought over, hung droopingly about me until I tied them in with a belt. Now-a-days my tall skinny figure would have fitted well present day fashion requirements but in those days a model needed to have curves.

When I was due to be discharged Colonel Bridges came in to see me for the last time. 'As you are the daughter of a Serviceman I have arranged for you to be classed as Army Family and not charged at our higher rates for non-military.'

'Thank you,' I replied, smugly proud that in such an exclusively military establishment they had a high regard for the Royal Navy. The inclusive bill including the ministrations of the Tapsalls, the medicament and the kippers all the way from Bombay, came to £100 for my seven weeks' sojourn. It seemed to me an enormous amount (which it was in those days) and a frightful waste of time and money.

I was borne by two bearers from the car into the Sialkot Residency in a carrying-chair, a mode of transport which I do not suppose exists any more. At least, I thought ruefully, it was one better than being carried out on a stretcher, and lots and lots better than being planted in the Padre's *godown!*

'*Ghussel taiyar* miss-sahib. *Malish*, miss-sahib?' Ayah beamed importantly bustling about to help me in my bath and massage my thin legs. Tappy came in once or twice to see that I was getting on all right. Tactfully and firmly she disentangled herself from my clutches and saw to it that I became independent of her. But although our close relationship was severed, she was never forgotten.

107

When I had been back only a few days there was an unexpected call from Stuart. He had broken his leg playing polo and would like to be put up by his sister.

'Oh, the poor boy,' was Sheila's sympathetic reaction. 'He won't be able to stay long though. In two weeks time we start back to Kashmir.'

'Might as well let him come and turn the ruddy place properly into a nursing home,' expressed Dem unable to resist the fun of having a dig at us all.

I knew he'd say it and he did: 'Great Scot, what have they done to your hair?' he asked on first sight of me as, wincing, he adjusted his crutches once out of the car to swing his way into the Residency.

'What have you done to *yourself*? You don't look too good,' I retorted.

'Tell us how it happened, old chap,' Dem wanted to know every detail. 'I didn't do anything. Some nincompoop got his stirrup caught in mine when I was riding him off,' Stuart told him. 'I felt the fibula snap, but of course no one on the field would believe me as there I was still sitting on the horse and writhing up and down in agony. They were furious when I refused to go on to finish the match. They wouldn't believe it could be anything more than a sprain.' ·

'I'd have thought they'd have put it in plaster,' Sheila said looking dubiously at the dangling leg.

'They haven't *got* any plaster-of-Paris in Risalpur,' Stuart said whilst steering himself into the drawing room with an agonized look on his face, 'I wish to goodness they had; the slightest movement...murder. All that idiotic MO did was to strap it up with tape with instructions not to put it to the ground.'

'Maybe you should have a second opinion. The Military Hospital here is jolly good.'

'No thanks, I've had enough of doctors.'

In the mornings we two sat around in the garden with our feet up on long chairs under the shade of the old banyan tree. We read the papers, did 'The Statesman' crossword and listened to cracked records played on Stuart's black portable gramophone as if we were in our nineties instead of 'in our prime' as they say. It was by now hot and overcast with a scorching wind blowing dust much of the time. The glorious clear-skied days of winter sunshine had come and gone when I was in hospital.

I became very fond of the old banyan tree. *It* could have told me many tales. It looked more like a pillared abode than a tree with its dozens of hanging branches like tentacles which had rooted themselves deep in the dry earth. Lying under its embracing arms and trunks I felt the garden to be as mysterious with its old trees as was the house. The peepul tree by the tennis court particularly fascinated me. The Hindu servants in the household believed it to be a holy tree full of spirits. One could certainly believe it even by daylight with its shiny leaves dancing and fluttering whitely in the wind. At night hordes of fireflies were attracted to it. They flitted like astral globes through its branches.

When it grew uncomfortably hot in the garden. Stuart and I would repair into the shuttered rooms of the Residency where the *chiks* rolled down over the verandahs had been sluiced with water and smelt delicious; where the overhead fans ruffled the enclosed air which became increasingly stuffy and stale as the day wore on. Stuart's record shrilled 'Your tiny hand is frozen' sung by Gigli seemed thoroughly inappropriate in that heat. 'Desert Song' was more to the point!

The two puppies were a delightful diversion. They played away with growls. They rolled each other over, nipping one another under our chairs with their sharp little teeth, their floppy too-large paws skidding on the loosely carpeted hall floor, the coolest and darkest room in the house. Every now and then there was a crash as they knocked over a table and sent objects flying - and not one of us had a whole pair of slippers left.

'Can't you control the dogs, Ronnie?' would come over plaintively from Sheila in her pent-house where she was having her afternoon siesta.

Daily and punctually at 3.30pm either Ram Singh or Hassan-ud-Din would drive up to the door to take the 'invalids' for an hour's drive which Sheila considered a necessity to broaden our outlooks stuck in the house day after day as we were. I really did feel ninety being driven slowly in stately manner along twisting dusty tracks with corrugated ruts in the flat country through villages where colourful women stood by the wells, and between bare fields and canals away from the noisy, honking, Grand Trunk Road.

One day I asked Stuart when he was going to marry his girl friend in England.

'Who told you?' he said abruptly.

'Sheila - and Ronnie. They said you were engaged.'

'Because I flew home on short leave last summer to see her doesn't mean we are on the point of getting married,' he replied witheringly. I found him a most exasperating man of few words, quite impossible to chat inconsequentialities with or to use the banter that went on with the young men in the Blue Church. If I made a flippant remark about a servant or a woman who was considered 'beyond the pale' in the cantonment, he just did not answer. I thought he was straight-laced to an absurd degree. He once saw me soaking an envelope to get off the stamp which had not been franked.

'That's not strictly honest', he remarked, not castigating me, but as a statement of fact. To me it was plain common sense not to waste the stamp! There were many things on which we did not see eye to eye, but it was no use trying to develop an argument on the subject because he would not argue! When I tackled him on this he said I was entitled to my own opinions and he would not presume nor want to try and change me. He had far too great a respect for me! Well, well; 'respect', and from a mature man like he? I still thought of myself as a girl with little brain out to see the world. However his remark made me think. Maybe during my brush with death I had grown up more than I knew.

· We were driven back from these daily drives to an enormous tea. Sheila was convinced that Stuart too needed feeding up, and I must say he looked gaunt and was in pain at the slightest movement. Dem was often out playing cricket in the heat, Ronnie with him to watch the match. Sheila who stayed in the cool of the old Residency, poured out the tea and told us the latest news heard on the wireless. The phoney war was still on, but children had been evacuated in large numbers to the country. She was worried about the boys and wondered if they should try and get them out earlier. The British Expeditionary Force was sitting in northern France and Belgium where there was 'nothing doing'. How long would this strange situation of being at war yet not fighting on the Western Front last?

'I knew she'd get her way in bringing the boys out,' Stuart said when Sheila was out of the room.

'What about you when you marry,' I asked, 'will you let your wife wear the trousers?'

'Not on your life,' Stuart smiled, 'I remember too well as a small boy being dominated by my big sister to ever let it happen again. She absolutely ruled both Keith and me!'

14
Return to Spring

The Sialkot Residency was being packed up; Stuart had to go back to his Mess where he would be well attended to by his bearer Nasrullah. On his penultimate day, I took him to see Tappy and to say goodbye to her myself.

The little nurse and the doctor entertained us right royally to tea in their small square house in the Civil Lines. Everywhere one looked there were photographs of their son from babyhood to manhood. In between were crammed knick-knacks, ivory ornaments, a sweet-smelling camphorwood chest, a brass tea-table on movable carved wooden legs and much other worked brass of tall candlesticks and vases. Garish religious prints decorated the walls.

The matching three-piece suite had lace antimacassars on the backs and arms which items were starched to a degree. Stuart kept on disarranging them and not knowing what to do when they fell off, one, I noticed with a smile, absentmindedly ending up in his pocket as a supposed handkerchief. But he was far from being a clumsy man and he managed to handle on his knee in a masterful way his teacup and small plate filled with pink cakes and curry sandwiches. His manner was charming and friendly and not in the slightest bit condescending as some elements in the cantonments were inclined to be with Anglo-Indians.

The dear Tapsalls looked unfamiliar to me in their own home. Dr Tappy wore khaki slacks and jacket. Tappy was dressed in a bright red garment rather too short for fashion, her crinkly hair left uncovered. Both of them obviously thought a lot of Stuart.

'A fine British soldier, a real gentleman,' Tappy said as I kissed her goodbye, 'you cannot do better than that.'

'He's not my type,' I frowned, 'and anyway he's got a girl in England.'

'What do you think of Stuart?' I asked Ronnie after he had left for Risalpur.

'He's all right,' she said puffing at her cigarette, 'he's good with dogs - got good hands.' Praise indeed from her. I had asked because I could not make him out. He had come into my room early on the day he left and woke me to kiss me goodbye with, 'hurry up and get really fit...' It was nice of him to have come in but no-one could have exactly called it a sisterly kiss... funny...

During our last day in Sialkot it was very quiet with the troops all out on manoeuvres. In the evening when the sun began to sink dark red with dust on the far horizon, even as one watched, it was gone. The house was thrown open, the chicks wound up, and the unforgettable fresh cool smell of the evening watering

111

on the hot still soil allowed to waft into the rooms. I wandered out into the garden to watch the *malis* unblocking the channelled water to let it flow and trickle in from one bed to another. They swished the dusty paths with wetted brushes made with twigs. Twilight is brief in India. It comes down in a few moments, so that one has to consciously stand and stare intensely to register the colours in one's memory as they rapidly change from red and orange to mauve and then that marvellous velvet black of the night.

The servants carried Ronnie's and my beds out onto the small lawn by the drive not far from the house but far out enough to be away from the hotness of the walls. They draped our mosquito nets over crossed poles. Ronnie and I came out in our dressing-gowns and slippers with Ayah waddling behind us. Her last duty of the day was to tuck each of us in so that no mosquito could penetrate from the outside.

It was a perfect moment, too lovely to allow oneself to go to sleep the moment one's head touched the pillow. Instead, in quiet voices we talked while we gazed up at the stars through the hazy folds of our white nets. The stars looked even larger and brighter than those I had viewed in Africa. They moved slowly across the firmament as we watched, though it was we that were moving. When the moon rose, the light was so bright that we took books out from under our pillows and read poetry to one another proving that one *could* read by moon-light.

Tomorrow I would be gone! Sialkot Residency had been cheated of this particular victim, thanks be, yet in a way I had grown fond of the creaking old house with its groans and moans, howls and eerie screams in the night following the fiendish laughter of the hyaenas. All the mystery that was there was borne out in the flitting shadows seen from our beds on the lawn by the dancing spirits in the peepul tree with their flickering glow-worm lights. Mutiny ghosts? The clack of their bones? Truly this was the real India of the plains, India of red dust, hotness, spices, relentless, uncaring, frightening, fascinating and always beautiful.

Tempered in the fire, petty irritations, clashes of character and flirtatious intent, all now seemed strangely superfluous.

I had come through to see the world in a new light.

🌴　　🌴　　🌴　　🌴

Slowly the Residency convoy snaked its way up the lower pass beyond Jammu to the valley of the Chenab. The frozen snow on the road made the ascent even more hazardous than four months previously. On this side of the Banihal Pass the scene was Swiss-like, picture-postcard with the hillsides dotted with *chir* firs covered in blobs of cotton wool and tinsel icicles.

A puncture brought the whole convoy to a slithering halt. We took the enforced stop to have our picnic lunch among the deodars at Batot where the long branches of the drooping pines were heavy with the weight of snow and the air was invigorating after the heat of the plains. The day was cloudy and there was no view of the high snow-blanketed mountains. There was only the wonderfully fresh air and the sound of the snow crashing down in white thumps from the deep forest of trees on either side.

We started off again, the cars revving and skidding, their chains clanking and crunching. We passed the Banihal Dak bungalow crammed with travellers, some of whom had already waited six days for the pass to be re-opened after an avalanche.

This time all was comfort for Ronnie and myself during the night spent up the Pass. We had VIP treatment in the superior PWD rest house which our party shared with Sir Peter Clutterbuck, head of the Forestry Department. *Farashes* (footmen) hastened to carry in our overnight cases for our bearers to make up our bedding rolls on the *charpoys*. I had been warned by Dr Tappy to watch it on the journey as the height might affect my heart adversely after the strain it had been put through by the high fever. Sensibly, after the excitements of the day, I retired to bed early. Rather than wash in the freezing *ghussel khana*, I ordered the tin tub to be brought in to my bedroom, and experienced one of the pleasures of a bygone Victorian age of indulging in a hip bath before a log fire, the soft glow of the oil lamps adding their enchantment of pretty shadows on the white-washed walls.

⚜   ⚜   ⚜   ⚜

The morning dawned brilliant as Dem, Sheila, Ronnie and I together with the Clutterbucks led the long convoy of stranded travellers on the forty-five mile drive to Srinagar. Emerging from the Banihal tunnel at its zenith we found nine foot banks of snow on either side dug out from the avalanche which had blocked the way. Slowly driving through the narrowly cleared track of road with room only for one-way traffic, we found gangs of coolies still hard at it moving the slush. They stopped working and stood aside to let us through.

Overhead, miles above the Vale, eagles glided in smooth circles looking for prey way below. On this clear day the infinite ranges stood out sharply against the blue sky. With the vast Kishtwar range to our right, the deep snow extended down to within a thousand feet of the lower level.

The first signs of spring became visible as we neared the bottom of the valley. At Verinag there were great strips of land carpeted with narcissus and orange lilies. Patches of water were edged with willow in their fresh yellowy green, beyond which cultivated land showed thin lines of light green where wheat sprouted. Here and there ponies with hobbled legs browsed on the marshland, and, close by as we sped along, I glimpsed clumps of yellow crocuses between counterpanes of creamy-blue violets and pale yellow primroses.

113

Kashmir side of Banihal Tunnel when opened after snow

All was colour too in the hamlets we passed where once again the women and children waved as they saw the flag on the bonnet. The picturesque tall-storied wooden farms showed up darkly against groves of pear trees covered in white blossom. The flat earth roofs of these houses made natural gardens of grass from which sprouted scarlet tulips. Through the winter the lower parts of the houses were crowded with sheep feeding on last year's iris and willow leaves; the warmth from the animal bodies rose to take some of the chill off the upper living rooms. Further on we came across orchards of quince trees with their delicate pink and white flowering petals unfurling. Then out in the open again we saw pretty little candy pink and white striped tulips alongside great mists of blue harebells.

It was all indescribably lovely and fresh after the heat of the plains, but the best moment for me was sweeping up the familiar Residency drive to be greeted by the red coated *chaprassis* and the half-dozen or so *malis* who stood in a row to welcome us. The dogs - only three left now since Stuart had taken Medlar back with him bounded out of the brake in barking exuberance at being released. Straight away Sheila and I toured the garden with growing exclamations of delight.

Under the great chenar trees, still devoid of leaves, a white carpet of large daisies grew on the lawn which looked wider and greener than ever in the unshaded light. In the formal bed by the drive were quantities of large-faced yellow and mauve pansies backed by rich cinnamon-red wallflowers of fragrant scent. By Ronnie's and my cottage on the drive (a brick building with a criss-crossing of wood in keeping with the Residency) grew a mass of stately orange Crown Imperial lilies fronted by hyacinths and anemones. In the herbaceous border, stocks and pinks were the first to bud beside a waxen flowered magnolia tree bare of leaves. In the rose beds leaf-shoots were bursting out in soft pinky browns. '*Shabash, shabash!*' Sheila praised the *malis* beaming round us, 'you have done a wonderful job. Well done!'

We hurried on to the orchard where we stood silently just looking. The apricot blossom was nearly over, but the peach trees formed clouds of mallow pink through which we could see the backcloth of the snow-fluted mountains. Here bloomed the mass of dainty pink-tinged apple blossoms, the almonds in pale cerise; the leaves of the walnut trees were just shooting, the cherry trees a riot of blossoms and beneath, the grass lay thick with butter-eyed narcissus and golden daffodils. The whole scene made a drift of dainty-coloured loveliness in the sunshine. Yes, it *was* more beautiful in its way, more ethereal, than the rich colours of lovely autumn.

Over by the summer-house, where later the yellow Fortune's rose cascaded so enchantingly, where ring doves cooed by their cot, and where now the banks were covered in crocuses, forget-me-nots and primroses, I dared to risk making a fool of myself, Sheila being the most undemonstrative person imaginable, and took her hand and squeezed it to show how happy I was to be there after the narrow squeak of the winter.

When we entered the Residency we found the *malis* had arranged flowers in every room in the house for our arrival. There were great bunches of mixed colours stiffly stuck into containers. We showed our appreciation and left the flowers as they were until they began to wilt.

❧　　❧　　❧　　❧

Sheila was to have her operation in May which gave me a few more weeks in which to get fit (as Stuart had instructed!), before taking over the running of the Residency with Ronnie. We were delighted with our tiny cottage. It had two bedrooms with sitting room between in which was a piano and a fireplace, the latter still much needed while there was a hoar frost in the early mornings. By noon it was warm enough to sit out in the sun. I was still supposed to rest a lot, and I took out a long wicker chair to place in a sunny spot to watch the birds. Sheila encouraged them by feeding them on the verandahs and with her help I learnt to distinguish their species for they did not all look like their British counterparts. The shiny-blue sparrows were recognisable, but the tom-tits of powder blue with canary yellow fronts were new to me as were the hoopoes and bulbuls. The former would come near as I lay still. They searched under my chair and in the bushes with their long beaks for grubs. They were fascinating to watch with their strikingly coloured sides and fine orange and sepia crests which they constantly fanned out and then let fall. The blue tits attacked the new leaf buds in the chenars, and though this caused a mess under the trees it made no impression on the multitude of new leaves that formed.

Most friendly of all were the charming little bulbuls with their coquettish top knots and red and yellow rumps. They came and tapped at the windows till we let them in. When the weather grew warmer and we had tea in the garden, these delightful birds would perch on the tea table and peck the sugar from the basin. Later arrived the green parrots with their long yellow tails, and the golden orioles, whose deep liquid notes trilled through the whole garden. These with their brilliant yellow and black forms could constantly be seen flashing like lightning from tree to tree.

Finally, and most exotic of all came the paradise flycatchers. They too were fascinating to watch. Their black heads and smokey-grey bodies seemed detached from their long white ribbony tails as they flew between the unfolding blossoms of the horse chestnut trees.

❧　　❧　　❧　　❧

With the fishing season in full swing and Sheila not well enough to go, I used to accompany Dem on his days out up the Dachigam Valley, the Happy

Cottage on the drive in Residency garden, Srinagar

117

Valley as the Kashmiris called it. We motored the twelve miles to Harwan, a lovely drive along the shores of the Dal Lake, clear and freshly filled with spring water. On the way we passed the Maharaja's Palace with lawn running down to the Lake, where I had taken tea with the Maharani who kept to semi-purdah. I found her a sweet and gentle person, easy to chat with.

Our road to the fishing took us behind the Nishat and Shalimar gardens now bright with the deep Persian purple of the Kashmir lilac which blended superbly with the heavy pink blossoms of the ornamental cherry trees. Everywhere one looked the walnut, poplar and mulberry leaves were bursting out. The hillsides were dotted with wild apricot, pear and almonds in full bloom leaving the ground around them white with fallen petals.

Dem suggested we stop at Harwan so that I could see its temple, once the home of a famous Buddhist saint. Nearby we had a look at a reservoir for the water supply of Srinagar. Here were tanks of fish hatcheries for trout breeding to stock the Kashmir rivers. The air smelt of fish which blotted out the scent from the yellow and mauve violets, anemones and cuckoo flowers which lay so thickly on the ground one could not avoid treading on them.

Once we reached the Dachigam river Dem disappeared upstream leaving me with a bearded *shikari* in a cotton checked coat who had instructions to teach me the rudiments of fishing. He put up my rod and had plenty to do for though I had been practising on the Residency lawn, here I was more often than not hooked into overhanging branches or caught up in knots from which he would painstakingly disentangle me. Enthusiastically I went on casting with my bright fly into the crystal-clear stream boiling with fish so that it was not through my skill that I soon found myself into my first trout, a most exciting and thrilling moment. But how to land it? I called for help to the *shikari*, who came running apparently as excited as I by the catch.

'Bahut accha, Miss-sahib,' he beamed, '*Khabadar*, be careful, *main jali lagaun*, wait for net. *Asti, asti!*' he objured me to reel in more slowly.

It felt as if I had a ton weight on the end of my rod and in my excitement I forgot his instructions and yanked the fish straight out onto the bank.

'Accha nahin, kabhi nahin, no good, no good AT ALL Miss-sahib,' my *shikari* evinced his displeasure.

However I *had* landed it and I was quite surprised to see how small was my spotted brown trout on the bank. When weighed it turned out to be not much over one pound, below which one threw them back. In this well stocked river, despite my tyro's thrashings, I soon caught more. My *shikari* jumped in hitching up his *dhoti* and still clad in his *chappals* (sandals), to net them. I had my quota of four in under an hour. Easy! The bag averaged under two pounds a piece.

Walking up river I found Dem round a bend. I sat on the bank to watch the expert at work. He stood deep, his grey flannel trousers sodden up to knee. In those days, no fishermen I knew wore boots. The clear jade-coloured water swirled past him in a pool. Intent and oblivious to everything else he watched his fly being gently carried down by the stream. Then once again he cast, his line making a pattern of silvery curves in the warm sunshine, his fly landing lightly, sinking in, carried down again and drawn across with consummate expertise until he struck into a nice fish. He kept catching them and throwing them back looking for bigger stuff. He would take his time for his four.

Climbing a little way up the hillside I settled down to wait among the wild flowers. I was in an Elysian miniature valley where bees busily buzzed and butterflies flitted past and landed with fluttering wings. I saw swallowtails, tortoiseshells, clouded yellows, cabbage whites and small blues which I was unable to name. In the distance I could see the Dal Lake, its Isle of Chenars lying serene, with the semi circle of mountains behind and the broad Jhelum River weaving its curving way through the green valley. From up here I could see how the Vale had inspired the country's craftsmen to paint the famous curving shawl patterns. It was a scene of utter peace, with just the sound of the rippling water, the humming of bees, a pi-dog barking in a nearby village, a shepherd boy above me calling to his flock of goats and sheep grazing amidst clumps of yellow barberry. I climbed further up the hill to investigate a great patch of white I had spotted. Could it be a sprinkling of snow so far down? No, it was not snow but a field of wild white roses. How right they were, I thought, to call this little valley of Palgham 'Happy Valley'.

Back home, which the Residency had become to me, the evening of that balmy day turned prematurely dark. There was a stillness about the garden and even the birds stopped their twitterings. I could hear claps of thunder among the mountains, claps which came nearer and nearer in hungry leaps until there were roars and huge bangs directly overhead in a blackness so great that the lights in the Residency had to be turned on. We watched through the windows as individual drops of heavy rain splashed down, lightning flashed and thunder roared directly overhead and the billowing black clouds released a deluge of hail stones the size of pigeon's eggs out of a giant's bucket to clatter down like stones on the shingle roof. Suddenly the house and lawn was covered in white. And it turned very cold.

Between showers next morning Sheila and I toured the garden to examine the damage. In a single hour all the delicate peach blooms, that crowning glory of the Kashmir spring, had withered. The outsize Dutch tulips and the stately Crown Imperials lay broken. It rained solidly for nearly two weeks with only glints of sunshine to light up the purple and white lilac, and the mass of irises from every shade of blue to mauve. Everything had been far advanced that spring of 1940 after what the Kashmiris considered a mildish winter. The weather was making up for it now!

But nothing could stop the flowers blooming in the Residency garden. The drive was soon lined with feathery spiraea, out there known as Indian May,

119

their long slender stalks tight with white buds. In no time the fragrant scent of lilies-of-the-valley surrounded us in our cottage, and Sheila was happy to find the strawberries she indulged in were in flower in their sheltered position by a high wall and had remained untouched by the storm.

With the air still fresh and the light translucent in its clarity, I decided to climb up the Takht-i-Suleiman, the thousand foot pinnacle which dominated the city, to test how fit I was. Kill or cure! The narrow path was very rough on this steepest of hills, and I took it slowly. On reaching near the summit I stood panting below the graceful Hindu temple atop until I got my breath back, and then I went on and up the steps which led into the sanctuary of a small room in the six foot thick walls containing a stone figure sitting in the lotus position. There was nothing else, no pilgrims, no trippers, just the idol and me and outside the mountains all around and the hum from the city below.

I sat on the steps for a while gazing at the view north-west to the smaller hill on which the Hari Parbat Fort sat squarely before the Dal Lake. Beyond lay the vaster grey Wular Lake, said to be the largest fresh water lake in Asia. Connecting the patches of water ran the long straight white road lined with thin poplar trees which, from my height, looked like match-sticks. Nicest of all was being able to look almost directly down into the Residency garden I knew so intimately. I could pick out the four chenar trees, and I saw the tiny figure of Ronnie coming out of the house and down the steps with the dots of the dogs romping before her. I rose to go back to my duties.

Lightly, as sure footed as in my childhood when in the native espadrilles I used to run down the donkey tracks in the Alpes Maritime, I ran down the Takht-i-Suleiman. As a child I had exulted in the feeling of flying down a mountain. Now I exulted in my new found fitness.

॥   ॥   ॥   ॥

Sheila was due to go into the little Nursing Home where George Ledgard would operate with Mrs Hempster and the other nurses in attendance. Before she went she and Dem had a confab with Ronnie and myself as to our future plans, which, before the war had started, was for her to take her puppy back to England, and me to resume my travels East. Ronnie's contract was already over; mine would be in July. The three boys were to be housed in the cottage. But now everything had changed, now Ronnie could not get a passage home, and even if she were able to nothing would induce her to leave Simon behind with the ban on pets on ships in wartime.

Ronnie and I were prepared. We had it all planned out. 'We've decided to share a houseboat,' Ronnie spoke up for us both. 'Mr Apcar is going to help us find one.'

'Good,' said Dem, 'I'm expecting to hear my next posting soon, but if I'm still here in the autumn you can come in twice or so a week and continue the good work for me…'

'…and help me with the flowers,' added Sheila. 'We wouldn't want either of you to feel we were kicking you out.'

When Ronnie had suggested sharing a houseboat, I thought it a very good idea. We got on well together in the cottage. It was fun entertaining our own friends there to tea, drinks and musical evenings round the piano. We knew that as miss-sahibs we would be much in demand with probably more invitations than we could cope with. We would find work - war work if there was any - and there was Mr Apcar and the dear old Canons to keep an eye on us if we needed someone to do so, and Drs Rawlence, Vosper and several other missionary ones to look after us if we were ill - which God forbid. It was all working out beautifully.... except, well.... it was only that, for me something was badly missing....

15
Gulmarg and a Royal Banquet

The war news from home throughout the winter and spring had been to us but a remote series of incidents as it had to the young officers in Sialkot who one and all were raring to go and who had put in, on the outbreak, to be transferred to the European front. They had been firmly told to stay put until called upon. Then all of a sudden young and old were galvanized by the sensational facts that the Germans were rapidly advancing through Holland and Belgium into France sweeping all before them including the British Expeditionary Force.

'Sounds like the Great War all over again,' groaned Dem on a visit to Sheila in hospital. She was sitting up in bed in one of 'Butterfly's' crèpe-de-chîne bed-jackets, two pigtails framing her pink cheeks. On her tray sat the dish of fresh strawberries I had brought her from the Residency garden, which fruit she was tucking into with gusto. Happily her operation had turned out to be less serious than expected and the surgeon had removed only her appendix.

'It says here that King Leopold of the Belgians has given in to the German demands without consulting his Government,' I read aloud from 'The Statesman'.

'Betrayed the Allies,' expressed Sheila in disgust, 'hope it won't upset our plans for the boys' bookings.'

'Shouldn't think so,' Dem grunted. 'It looks as if France will be the next to go. Very serious. I'll wire Delhi for instructions about cancelling the annual Garden Party.'

We did so on our return to the Residency. 'Carry on as normal. Our policy is to show the Indians we are in control and not panicked by the situation,' the signal came back.

'Humn. *Tamasha* as usual. Seems all wrong, somehow. Better get on with it, Evelyn,' Dem said with a grimace.

So when Sheila was home again the Garden Party was held as France fell and the British Army was being hounded to the Channel all the way from Dunkirk and Calais to Cherbourg with the saga of the fleet of little boats (my father, called up out of the Reserve, was one of them), who set out to rescue as many as they could, which turned out to be more than anyone believed to be possible, though most of the equipment was lost.

Killing and destruction, wounding and tragedy.... where was war? The scene in the Residency garden was idyllic. Tables were dotted about in the shade of the chenar trees. *Khitmagars* waited on the company and served fragrant

China tea with lemon, thinly cut well-peppered cucumber sandwiches together with small iced cakes and de Souza's speciality of a deliciously moist walnut cake. After this came bowls of the prolific crop of home grown strawberries with lashings of whipped cream.

Groups of ladies in flowing dresses, long white gloves up to elbows and picture hats worn at an angle, strolled with men in morning coats and top hats to admire the herbaceous borders where towering delphiniums eight foot high bloomed gloriously in shades from dark to light blue. These were backed by trellis-work on which the rose of Kashmir tumbled in a mass of pink, the whole picture framed by the silvery-green of a tall blue cedar.

Indian gentlemen in milk-white jodhpurs with apricot brocaded coats and *pugris* a-glint with gold, stood with wives graceful in their floating saris in rainbow shades as varied as those of the clarkias, aquilegias, and larkspurs in the borders. HH's military band played popular tunes round the tall flag pole from which the Union Jack proudly fluttered as if it had not a care in the world.

※   ※   ※   ※

With the holiday season now in full swing, and with a deluge arriving up for a break from the hot weather in the plains, every houseboat, hotel and boarding house became full to bursting. Many were friends from Sialkot including the faithful Blue Church boys with James, and 'Little John' with whom I felt an affinity, both having had 'our brushes with death' and come through. With Allister Trainsh, Barney Barrow, Jim Middleton and Arthur Falkenor there were leisurely *shikara* picnics followed by bathing from the anchored rafts out by Nagim Bagh, the day ending with cocktail parties on houseboats, dinners and dances at Nedou's or the Club. I made a good friend of another girl up there, Kate Bromhead, and I had some proposals, one from an extremely good looking young man in the Forestry Service, aptly named Forest Elvers, met through the Clutterbucks. Few could understand why I turned him down. I could scarcely understand it myself except that my illness had changed me.

One of the most enjoyable of days was spent with Sheila and Dem watching the Tyndale-Biscoe Church Missionary schoolboys and girls at their water sports followed by a compulsory three mile swim across the Dal Lake and then a climb up a nearby 13,000 foot mountain.

The contrast between these healthy boys and the life most Indians led a stone's throw away from the school, had worried me when I first came to Kashmir. I, like practically everyone else in my position, other than the saints such as Mother Teresa of Calcutta and the missionary doctors, nurses and teachers, had to find some way of coming to terms with the poverty all around. There was no doubt that after the first shock of seeing the festering sores, the limbless beggars, the tiny children leading the blind, one became accustomed,

123

or was it hardened? I remembered meeting some Americans who on viewing the poverty in Bombay had caught the next boat back. We, who worked out there and were caught there by war, had no alternative but to stay, and in staying we became used to the situation, used to seeing the sights, hardened perhaps but still left with a sense of helplessness in the face of the hordes of millions living in misery. We did what we could in our own little circle by treating our retainers well, giving a home to their families and all the 'hangers on' who went with them, and saw that they were fed and housed. Little enough, but I comforted myself that, incredibly, most of the people survived. I developed an enormous admiration for them. From when I first took in the population on the station platforms in Bombay - after my panic at the Docks - I almost envied them in their family groups. Dost Mohammed showed me their humour. What could one do but laugh with them? Ayah and I were always laughing. She took everything in her stride. In Kashmir I came across marvellous contrasts of faithfulness and fickleness, of loyalty and roguishness. At times they were incredibly hardworking, at others purposely indolent. And they were generous. The poor gave alms to the poorer. As I once wrote in my 'Characters of the British Raj' they were resilient in adversity, and they were wise with wisdom that had nothing to do with education. They may have lived herded together, but each was very much an individual. Each one was a character....

❦   ❦   ❦   ❦

After the Garden Party, and to complete Sheila's convalescence, Dem decided on a short trip up to the summer Residency in Gulmarg. Ronnie stayed behind with the dogs. We three drove to the road-head at Tangmarg where Sheila and I mounted *tats* (sturdy mountain ponies) while Dem walked with the pony men. The path twisted and turned its way in steep gradients between forests of pine trees, spruces and cedars. The ground was carpeted with pine needles which gave out their pleasant aromatic smell and muffled our ponies' footfalls. The only sound on the still, hot air was that of the rushing water from the mountain stream the path followed.

Some thirty miles from Srinagar, beyond a ridge in a saucer-shaped valley, and 8,500 feet above sea level, we arrived in the hill resort of Gulmarg. The Kashmiri shepherds called it the 'Meadow of Flowers' where they brought their sheep, cattle and ponies to graze in the summer amongst the giant columbines, the blue Jacob's Ladders and the mauve salvias growing in the basin in as much profusion as in any Swiss pasture.

The village of Gulmarg consisted of Nedou's Hotel with its pine log cabins near the golf links, some hutted shops, and many bungalows most of which had khaki tents erected in their compounds for the overflow of visitors.

The summer Residency had once been the old Parsonage. It lay a little way out from the village on a meandering level track running along the outer lip of

124

Gulmarg Residency

the basin. The path to it had a steep drop to one side; the other side was fringed with a mass of bell-shaped blood-red rhododendrons. The house itself was a chalet-type bungalow with steep roof against the heavy snows of winter. At the rear were a series of guest huts, each standing on its own, one of which I luxuriated in with my own sitting room. The main building was built of wooden planks on a sturdy stone base, carved edgings round the low eaves. Elaborately moulded banisters to the fore overlooked the pathway - not a main one and therefore little used - from where could be seen one of the most spectacular views in India.

The Ferozepur Nullah, a small heavily forested valley, dipped straight down from the path some two thousand feet to a turbulent river of fishing fame of that name. Far away in the plain could be seen the Wular Lake and the hazy outline of Srinagar. Directly across the valley lay a fabulous view of the Himalayas dominated by the great massif of Nanga Parbat, the 'Naked Maiden', or 'Veiled Virgin' as the locals translated because more often than not a puff of blown snow or a wisp of cloud hid her several summits. There she rose eighty miles away, 26,650 feet high and looking as if one could touch her in her glittering, eternally snow-capped glory. She became my very favourite mountain, one I likened to a picture all my own. To draw back my bedroom curtains early in the mornings to see how she was that day and view her again in all her majestic glory was an experience out of this world. I would watch the ever-changing lights on her face and see the defusions of pink and yellow light up her shape. Edged with silver against the sky, I watched the colour turn to rosy red with puffs of snow pluming up in the wind like white ostrich feathers. Then in the evenings the unforgettable brilliant sunsets fading away from crimson to a modest blush. I knew her contours so well that forty years later when I flew over Nanga Parbat, I was able to pick her out straight away from the other mountains.

But one could not gaze at Nanga Parbat all the time, and sometimes she was invisible when wreathed in cloud. There were other sights to see higher up in the keener mountain air. Here walking up to where the distant glacier of Apharwat glistened and snow drifts still lingered on the northern slopes, Sheila and I found ourselves back in spring in shaded copses carpeted with aconites and rare orchids. We followed a torrent through woods of blue pine, and crawled on hands and knees over tree-trunk bridges spanning swollen waterfalls, and stopped to paddle like children in pools of icy water where delicate maidenhair ferns grew out of rocks, marine-blue gentians peeped, and most rare of all the sky-blue Meconopsis Baileyi, or Himalayan poppy, flowered.

Though we had difficulty in tearing ourselves away to continue the season in the heat below, I had been invited together with Ronnie to stay up here for August, the hottest month, and, *insh'allah* (as Dost Mohammed would have said) I would be back again in the Summer Residency with its magnificent view of Nanga Parbat.

The drawing room, Gulmarg Residency

There was an embossed card awaiting us below, an invitation for the Residency party to join Hari Singh and his gentle Maharani for an evening 'picnic' in the 'Abode of Love'. This was the Shalimar Bagh of 'Pale Hands I Loved' fame to the British. For this private royal evening party the garden was closed to the general public.

The lake was full to the brim from the melting snows; the lotus plants bloomed in great clusters of pink flowers framed by their large polished leaves. The sun was setting in a fiery glow as our *shikara* came to rest near a trailing willow tree by a landing stage lit with swinging lanterns.

We were greeted by our hosts, and in the fading light toured the garden, sometimes named the 'Cherry Garden' for the beauty of its blossom in spring. It was the most royal of the gardens, a great favourite of the Moghul Emperor Jahangir who called it 'A paradise within a paradise'. It was secluded, tucked away from the lake by the canal, with a black marble pavilion added by Shah Jahan and set in a long tank from where jets of water rose up to splash into the foundations.

In this black pavilion sat a group of HH's court musicians playing their twanging zithers. The site was serenely calm and peaceful with gentle streams running through the slight incline. The garden had been laid out by Jahangir in the seventeenth century in a simple design which divided it into sections representing the eight parts of paradise, a paradise built for his 'Light of the World', none other than Nur Jahan, the daughter of Itmad-ud-Daula, whose superb mausoleum lies a few miles north of the Taj Mahal.

Our party, with Sheila, Ronnie and I in long evening dresses, together with the other guests drifted down through the central part, where all that was left of the Audience Hall were the foundation stones, to the lower section by the grey-marbled pavilion where we were served with pink champagne. By now the light had faded and the garden was lit up with hundreds of tiny yellow oil lamps outlining the central stream. The lights flickered warmly in contrast to the brilliant and steely lights from the stars appearing overhead. Slowly a full moon rose to fill the garden with an alabaster light beside deep shadows cast by the pavilions.

On this select evening 'picnic' we were few in number, only about thirty guests in all and greatly outnumbered by servants, one of whom was a food taster for HH who was nervous of being poisoned and often insisted on cooking for himself. Although the Maharani was not in strict purdah, she still only attended small private parties of carefully selected guests if the company was mixed. We felt honoured to be invited that evening when all the other guests were Indian, the men colourful in their silk salwars, the ladies like butterflies in their shining

Ayesha Cooch Behar arriving at the Residency
(engaged to Maharaja of Jaipur as his third wife)

129

saris. The Maharani never came to the Residency with HH on the few occasions he did, such as the recent Garden Party, but Sheila was hoping to get her to a 'ladies only' tea party in return for her hospitality to us.

Despite these restrictions Her Highness appeared perfectly at ease in mixed company at their party when smoothly she introduced us to her brother and to the Maharaja of Jaipur and his fiancée, the younger sister of the Maharaja of Cooch Behar, whom they called Ayesha, who was destined to become the polo playing Jai's third wife.

She was a most beautiful girl of sixteen with shoulder length black hair flowing freely. Her sari clung gracefully to her youthful figure below which peeped dainty manicured feet clad in sandalled shoes. She wore a diamond of large size on her engagement finger. For those times she was a modern girl, not brought up in purdah, and with advanced ideas on women's rights. She was obviously radiantly happy and adoring of her fiancé - and he her - who was a star of Indian polo players, playing to a handicap of nine at the age of twenty-two.

For this exclusive party we sat on the lower terrace at small tables ironed into their starched tablecloths to be served by the fleet of red turbaned *khitmagars* to a four course meal. All was smoothly organized by the ADCs, with Hari Singh and his Maharani moving unobtrusively round the tables. I found myself sitting in turn with the Maharani and then with HH himself who at one point sat down heavily beside me after an Indian ADC, seeing him approach, had hastily risen to vacate his chair. 'You know all about me,' HH teased. 'I gather you type the letters to me. All this silly fuss,' he went on as he handed over his plate to the food-taster at his elbow to sample.

'Dem tells me you like to cook for yourself, Your Highness,' I ventured.

'Quite so, Miss Hart. Often I cook. I enjoy it. If I were not the Maharaja of Kashmir I would be a chef!' he bantered. The rest of the company, who had been listening in, seeing that HH was in great form, laughed heartily at the joke.

When Sheila deemed it was time to leave we said our farewells and were escorted to the Vauxhall waiting for us on the road higher up.

'Some picnic!' observed Sheila. 'I don't know when I've enjoyed myself so much.'

'Hear, hear. Can't see anything anti-British about HH.' I agreed as we were driven off.

'Better, much better. Polo, cricket, the shooting and Sheila have helped to thaw him,' Dem declared taking his wife's hand.

'Well, I for one will never forget the fairy-tale evening,' I sighed contentedly, starry eyed about it all.

'It's the pink champagne what's done it,' laughed Ronnie, 'I feel quite rosy myself!'

130

16
Farewell the Enchanted Vale

By now it had turned very hot in Srinagar, daily between 85° and 95° F in the shade. Flies galore drowsily zizzed on the windows of the cottage. Lethargically Ronnie and I swatted at them.

The coolest part of the day was in the morning. I rose early to do the flowers after which we breakfasted on the lawn under the nearest chenar tree. The *chaprassis* had carried out a carpet and placed a table with white tablecloth upon it. Sitting there eating our porridge - Dem always had to have porridge for breakfast with cream whatever the temperature - and then bacon and eggs or rumble-tumble as the bearers called scrambled eggs, with toast and marmalade to follow and plenty of coffee, the three dogs lying by, it looked and felt exactly as if we were feeding in a leafy dining-room. It was a wonderful time of day, and still the flowers in that garden bloomed. Now there were amazingly tall hollyhocks and Canterbury-bells in the herbaceous borders, backed by giant sun-flowers. Sweet-williams, gladioli, geraniums, canna-lilies, eschscholtzias and dahlias flowered abundantly in other beds.

The *malis* were constantly at it hoe-ing, tie-ing up, and watering. The spray from the hoses made drifts of rainbow vapour over the lawns. From the fruit-garden came raspberries and peaches with ripe cherries for the picking. To scare the birds off the cherry trees, one or other of the *malis* stayed stationed there night and day. Quantities of mulberries dropped onto the ground making black messes, and in the vegetable garden, as if we did not have more than enough flowers already, Sheila grew her favourite sweet peas staked in straight rows, each shoot tied and cut so as to allow only one stem's growth which truly produced the maximum bloom.

The mail was brought daily on a tray for Dem to sort out, usually delivered at lunch by which time we were sitting in the comparative coolth of the house with overhead fans going full speed. This was a time when even the birds in the garden had given up twittering and were asleep.

'What, not ANOTHER,' Dem would exclaim with mock wit as he recognized his brother-in-law's handwriting. He would turn it over several times and pretend to scrutinize the postmark and date before handing it over to me with, 'I can't think what *he's* got to write to you about!'

'Mostly about his horses', I answered defiantly.

'He only writes to me when he wants to come and stay,' Sheila declared in a peevish voice.

131

Our correspondence had started on my return to Srinagar. Stuart's leg soon mended and he was back in the saddle again with his troop and playing polo. His letters were friendly, even affectionate as if I were a younger sister in the family, but nothing more. They were interesting, about his life as a bachelor in the Mess, the friends in his *chummery* bungalow, his men, manoeuvres. Never a mention of his girl friend in England. I had no idea what the situation was there. He seemed to like writing to me, and I wrote back weekly telling him of our doings and how Sheila was getting on after her operation.

So, when the letters ceased and he turned up in Srinagar in June in a grey second-hand Chevrolet with his bearer Nasrullah, and Medlar in tow - much grown - for three weeks' fishing leave, I did not know what to expect, or if to expect anything. But on seeing him again, deeply bronzed by his out-of-door life, I knew what *I* felt.

The news from home, endlessly listened to and discussed, could not have been worse. The British had been driven into the sea; thousands had been taken prisoner; Belgium had been overrun by the Germans yet once again; France had surrendered and was mostly occupied, and in the Far East the Japanese, having romped down China, appeared bent on entering Burma. India next? What were *they* up to? Sitting under the chenar trees having a full English breakfast it was all hard to assimilate. Yet it *was* true. The conversation now concentrated on the miracle of the small boats that had saved so many; about the bombing after which the phoney war had started up in earnest, and the determination to fight on alone.

'We'll have another go at them. Thank God for the Channel,' Dem said.

'We'll beat 'em all right - in the end...' Stuart declared ominously.

But life in Kashmir still carried on much as before. The men went out fishing whilst Ronnie and I went ahead with our plans for a house-boat at the end of the month. Stuart dropped a remark one day that he was fed up with people who shilly-shallied, a reference, I presumed, to his girl friend. Obviously he was the sort of man who was never going to come to the point - with me at any rate. 'Too bad,' I hardened my heart and accepted another invitation from Forest.

🌻   🌻   🌻   🌻

A few days later Dem, Sheila and Stuart were due to go fishing up the Trikka, a small river that was HH's preserve and therefore a somewhat special venue and said to be seething with trout. I was rather sorry that I had not been invited. I would have liked to see it.

Late on the evening before, Stuart approached me. 'Dem's pulled out for tomorrow,' he said airily, 'and Sheila's going to have a day resting after another of her giddy fits. Her op doesn't seem to have cleared that up. Pity to waste a rod. What about you coming, that is if you can get up at five?'

'Of course I can,' I declared defensively.

132

'Good. Don't be late. Mustn't miss the first rise.'

I managed it, and we set off in the Chevrolet in the dark plus all the gear. Just short of a village, Stuart stopped the car. I had never been driven by him before and was glad to find he drove well if fast. What now, I thought. Was there something wrong with the engine?

He turned to me on the front seat beside him, with: 'Will you marry me?'

'Yes,' I replied before he could change his mind or shilly-shally or whatever.

'Good,' he said and briefly kissed me on the lips before driving on.

I laughed because it was such a funny way of proposing and not a bit romantic as I had imagined, and also because I found myself blissfully happy.

'I suppose we're engaged? Fancy having a proposal of marriage at five-thirty in the morning. I should think it is unique. Why now? Why not before? I mean when we were...'

'Carefully planned. You were in no state to know your own mind in Sialkot. It would not have been fair. As to this morning, if you'd said 'yes'; fine. If you'd said 'no' I'd still have had a whole day's fishing to take my mind off it!' he said looking happy too.

'You're impossible.'

'I don't much like being hurt.'

'Who does?'

'There we were behaving like ancient old crocks, me with my broken limb, you recovering from death's door having given me a fearful fright when Sheila wrote that you were dangerously ill.'

'A fright; really?'

'Yes really! As I was saying, there we were going on as if we were a hundred being taken for stately drives by Hassan-ud-Din. I thought if we could get on so well as inactive invalids, a situation in which I would normally have been frustrated and bored, instead of which I was enjoying your company more than I ever had with another girl...'

'More than with the one in England?'

'Don't interrupt...then this was the stuff for a heady marriage, in other words we'd experienced what 'for worse' was like, so it could only be 'for better' in future!'

'You didn't answer my question,' I purred.

'Oh, didn't I? She and I started off on the wrong foot there, pressurized by four parents who were dead keen. They thought it was time I got married and how nice it would be for *them*. So the answer to your question is that I enjoy your company, darling, far, far more than the other girl's.' Thereupon Stuart took my hand on a bend, and it was just as well there was no traffic on the lower Liddar road at that time of day or we'd have ended up in the ditch. As it was we did stop the car then... for a moment.

133

After that the Chev climbed on up two thousand feet to the Trikka which was everything it was reputed to be, a beautiful dancing little river seething with brown trout. The road came to an end by a forest bungalow situated on its own just above the river and to the east of the hamlet. We disgorged from the car and looked about us. The bungalow was in a most enchanting setting with the river running past, the mountains glimpsed high above the trees, and in front of the house grew a natural wild garden untouched by human hands, a garden of yellow and mauve violets, anemones and cuckoo flowers. Paradise indeed.

'Perfect for a honeymoon?' Stuart asked with raised eyebrow.

'Oh yes,' I nodded soft-eyed. 'It belongs to the Forestry Department. Dem told me to look out for it. I'm sure he could fix it with Sir Peter Clutterbuck.'

'Come on,' said Stuart. 'Mustn't miss the morning rise.'

Later with our catch laid out beside us, and while eating our picnic, we talked non-stop. 'I'll have to get extension of leave - shouldn't be difficult - so that we can have ten days honeymoon or so here before we go to the Staff College.'

'Where's that? What for?'

'Quetta. To be trained as a Staff Officer, goose,' Stuart said amused at my ignorance. 'There'll be a married quarter for us. *Wana* huts to sleep in outside since the 1935 earthquake which cracked the walls of most houses there. My syce will have to go ahead with my polo ponies by train. Nasrullah will fix all that up.'

'I shall miss Ayah.'

'Let's take her and her brood! Her husband can be my *Havildar*. I need an orderly to look after my uniform.'

'Will Dem mind?'

'Shouldn't think so. He can have his pick round here.'

'Oh lord. Ronnie. I'd forgotten all about her. We were going to share a houseboat.'

'Well, I'm not having Ronnie sharing our *Wana* hut. You'll have to choose between us!'

🌴   🌴   🌴   🌴

On our return to the Residency we rushed up to Sheila's bedroom with our news.

'Got your quota of fish?' she asked from her bed.

'Rather,' said Stuart, his arm about me, 'and I caught a whale!'

Sheila was delighted and Dem came in with a bottle of champagne and a grin all over his face to such an extent I began to wonder if they had not planned it all along. Ronnie, thank goodness, didn't burst into tears but took it on the chin. I told her I was sorry to let her down. She replied that she'd share the house-boat with Kate Bromhead who was looking round for somewhere to live. Her

134

Forest bungalow - 'perfect for a honeymoon'

135

generosity came to the fore in that she was genuinely pleased for both Stuart and myself; she agreed to be my maid-of-honour.

Things moved fast, and had to, after that red-letter day out in the Trikka Valley. Stuart cabled his Commandant for permission to marry and for extension of leave for the honeymoon. Both requests were granted. Congratulations poured in, one from my father in England (called up out of the Reserve, he was in charge of sweeping the Thames of the new magnetic mine), another cable from Stuart's parents in Malta, another from Keith and Joan whom I'd met in the autumn when they had come down to stay from Gilgit on their way to another posting. Canon Stokoe agreed to marry us, and we fixed the date for the wedding for exactly three weeks ahead to give time for the banns to be read. He gave us a private talk full of wisdom and sound advice which stood us in good stead for the 'pack and follow' years to come.

Invitations were hastily drawn up and produced by the printer on the Bund. De Souza started straight away on a two-tiered wedding cake. Sheila decided to make up my bouquet herself from flowers in the garden. 'Fluffy' Best, a young widow, née Tyndale-Biscoe with whom I had struck up a friendship, and who in dire need had started a dress shop on the Bund, designed and made my wedding dress. This caused problems to begin with as there was no damask or satin material to be had in white or cream in Srinagar, nor was there any time to order some from Calcutta or Bombay. In the end Fluffy and I decided on chiffon as the only solution for white. 'Butterfly' made up a trousseau of nighties and underclothes, otherwise I had enough garments brought out from England to go on with. Mary, the wife of 'Bunny' Fry, who had taken over from the Dixons, undertook to do the flowers in Church, and Stuart had a carved jade stone bought in the bazaar set in gold for me to wear while we were engaged. He promised a 'proper' diamond engagement ring from Hamilton's of Calcutta later, and was as good as his word.

Then came the first bit of friction. I wanted a platinum wedding ring to go with the modest jewellery I possessed, but Dem, unexpectedly, kicked up a row about this. He declared he would not give me away unless I was 'decently' married with one of gold. Impasse, in which Stuart refused to take sides. Just when things were coming to boiling point, nerves fraying, the little jeweller on the Bund came to the rescue by suggesting white gold at which the burra-sahib could not quibble. Meekly Dem agreed at which I began to wonder if it had not been a huge leg-pull to disconcert me? In which case he had certainly succeeded.

Feeling distinctly unbalanced by the whole pressing palaver of a slap-up wedding in so short a time, on looking through the marriage service to be I myself quibbled at saying 'obey' which seemed to me too archaic for words. What would happen if he went mad or something? I had never had need to obey or disobey a man in my woman-ridden life and was not going to start to now. Canon Stokoe said that was quite all right by him and that he often omitted those words

136

on request, and Stuart said he could not care less whether I obeyed him or not as long as I did the 'till death do us part' bit, which I thought was so sweet and broadminded of him I would have 'obeyed' him on the spot!

Sheila, recovered from her latest indisposition, took over total and majestic control. Talk about obeying. I had no say in the wedding arrangements whatsoever! Soon, in the hectic time that followed, I became too tired to care anyway. Presents of walnut furniture, Kashmiri crafts, Hadow's rugs, Chinese lacquer-ware, dinner sets, Indian silverware, linen and blankets from Elgin Mills and many cheques began to pour in, all of which I managed to acknowledge in thank-you letters before the wedding. HH Sir Hari Singh, who had expressed his desire to attend the Reception (but naturally not in his high caste the church ceremony), sent us a sterling silver cigarette box. There were cables of congratulations galore including a special one from the Tapsalls.

The servants were as excited about the nuptials as all of us, and rushed around spring cleaning and polishing until the whole of the Residency smelt of linseed floor polish, and the four dogs skidded on the rugs more than ever. By this time I had become totally exhausted and snapped at Stuart. The men, deciding the whole female momentum was too much for them, disappeared to fish up the lower gorged Liddar and did not re-appear until two days before the wedding by which time I was in a panic lest there should be no bridegroom at all.

❦   ❦   ❦   ❦

Sheila had decided that for my last night in the Residency I should go back into my old room. It was a night reminiscent of the one in the Sialkot Residency only without the headache - when I had not slept at all. I was far too excited to sleep now, and it was very hot. Sleeping pills, powders or any sort of calmative were unheard of in those days outside of hospital. My old room seemed strange and vast after the cosiness of the Cottage I had shared with Ronnie. In the early hours of the morning I wandered out into the balcony in search of cooler air. The *chowkidar*, whose snores I had listened to through the long night, had already folded his blanket and left. Doubts assailed me. I was far too tired to get married. I did not really know Stuart all that well. What sort of speech would he make? Would he stumble over the words to cover me with embarrassment? *Why* had I ever said 'yes' in such a hurry?

At last came Ayah's welcome tap on the door. She entered bearing *chota hazri*. Hot on her heels arrived Sheila with strict orders, none of which were welcome. I was to stay in bed for breakfast and rest. Dost Mohammed would bring in my tray in due course. I was not permitted to get up before eleven o'clock after which a light lunch would be brought to my room.

'This is ridiculous. What is Stuart doing?' I protested enviously. I knew that he with Dem and the best man, Paul Gambier, a married Captain in the Royal

Signals whose wife was in England having a baby, who had arrived up to stay with us for the event, had gone to the Club and had probably had a rare old time while there was I...

'Having breakfast downstairs. You are not allowed to leave your bedroom lest you meet him.'

'Why on earth shouldn't I meet him?'

'My dear child, you must not see your husband-to-be, or he you, on your wedding day before you meet in church. Custom decrees it would be unlucky to do so.'

I could only surmise that Sheila was repeating the outline she had gone through on *her* wedding day in the twenties in a relic of past centuries.

The morning dragged on. At last I rose to bathe and dress, after which I partook of my solitary lunch in my dressing-gown. Bug-eyed with lack of sleep and nerves, I toyed with the food set before me and vowed if I ever had a daughter I would not impose such ridiculous restrictions. I then spent some time putting on make-up in an endeavour to cover the pools under my eyes.

Ronnie came in like a breath of fresh air and all of a sudden it was bustle if not actual hurry to get dressed in time. We were late and the long sleeved chiffon dress had innumerable fiddly little cloth-covered buttons to be done up all the way down the back. My veil attached to a Juliet cap was adjusted. Finally Sheila came in to inspect the result and to hand me her bouquet of cream-coloured dahlias and white carnations. At long last, when all was clear and Stuart and Paul had left for the church, I was permitted to descend the staircase, my short train sweeping its immaculate surface behind me. Below, in the hall, the servants were lined up to wish me well.

Ayah was there full of dimples, her upright *Havildar* husband beside her. All had been arranged for them to come and work for us. On our return from honeymoon the *Havildar* would drive the Chev the long way to Quetta via Lahore and through the arid and, at that time of year, boiling hot Sind Desert while the horses and rest of the party went by train with the packing cases. Nasrullah, 'Nasru' to me now, a rotund bearer, who Sheila had declared to be fat and lazy with not enough work to do with his bachelor employer taking his meals in the Mess, (that was all going to change with a memsahib in charge) had gone ahead with a lorry carrying our bedding and provisions plus a *khansama* to cook, a *bhisti*, a *chowkidar*, the sweeper and Medlar to the Trikka Forest Lodge to prepare for our coming. But there in the line was Dost Mohammed giving me a trace of a smile beside beaming de Souza and de Mello. Punctually at ten to three Sheila and Ronnie were driven off.

Even though I was bursting with heat, and the temperature that day registered 94° F in the shade, Dem declared that I looked pale and gave me some neat brandy as we stood in the hall. He took a swig himself. So even the Resident in Kashmir felt the tension of the occasion! And then we were off in the

HH Sir Hari Singh arriving for the wedding, escorted by the Resident

The bride and groom welcome guests under the shamiana in the Residency garden

beribboned Vauxhall driven by the ever impassive Hassan-ud-Din. Out of the Lodge gates, flag flying, the guards saluting, up the main road and into the short drive we went, the Cross of St George hanging limp in the breathless air of the midsummer's day, as we came to rest before the ivy-clad portals of All Saints' Church.

Dem's whispered witticisms were comforting as we entered the west door of the packed little church, and for the first time I caught sight of my husband-to be in uniform of light gaberdine, sword, shining cross belt, highly polished boots and a navy-blue and green Frontier medal glimpsed as he turned to watch me approach. His uniform brought it home to me that the man I was marrying was very much an army officer, and not just Sheila's brother heretofore only seen in mufti. He was a stranger standing there beside me as the service began and we repeated the vows. But by now my full attention was drawn to the Canon. Fascinated I watched in the hushed silence of the flower-filled church the drops of sweat, one by one, trickling down Canon Stokoe's rubicund face to drip into his surplice.

❦   ❦   ❦   ❦

Back in the Residency garden, the scarlet-liveried *chaprassis* opened the Vauxhall's door by a strip of crimson carpet over the lawn leading to a small, scalloped *shamiana* tent of many colours where we stood to shake hands with the guests. No member of my family was present, so that I was particularly pleased to welcome Mrs Fitzmaurice Acton on holiday up there, who knew my father. To make up for this lack there were many new found friends, including the diminutive Frys, the Baileys, Captain Ledgard and Mrs Hempster, a Mrs Baily whose husband was Political, dear Mr Apcar, of course, with Kate, Fluffy and Major Hadow. Of the Indian element I had come to know there was Sirdar Effendi and Sahibzada Sir Abdussamad Khan who came with the Rani of Jasdan. There was Sir Peter and Lady Clutterbuck with Lady Roberts and Colonel Muir, and our old friends the Bishop of Lahore and Mrs Barnes who were on leave in Srinagar as were Doc Holland with Lady Holland whom we were to see much of in Quetta, and we had invited the whole of the choir. There was a pause from handshaking after greeting the Prime Minister of Jammu and Kashmir State, while all waited for HH who then arrived in a limousine with his Staff and Aide, and the proceedings could begin.

It was all going smoothly as the champagne flowed and tea was tucked into under the deep shade of the chenar trees where we cut de Souza's beautifully decorated cake with Stuart's unwieldy sword. But still I felt nervous as the speeches began with Dem who spoke easily and mentioned all the right people including my father and Stuart and Sheila's parents so far away. I caught Ronnie dabbing her eyes with a handkerchief; and then I heard Stuart's voice beside me:

141

'Your Highness, your Honour, ladies and gentlemen, my wife and I would like to thank you…'

He spoke well and with humour. Like so often I need not have worried. It was all going to be all right!

And in this happy way I entered the biggest adventure of my life.